I0088169

In His Presence

By: Jacqueline T. Flowers

Foreword By: Jerry W. Flowers, Sr.

Llumina
Christian
Books

Unless otherwise indicated, all scripture quotations are from the King James Version of the Bible.

IN HIS PRESENCE
ISBN 0-9634196-1-7
COPYRIGHT 1993 BY JACQUELINE T. FLOWERS

PUBLISHED BY JACQUELINE T. FLOWERS
P. O. BOX 671522
HOUSTON, TEXAS 77267-1522

Printed in the United States of America. All rights reserved under International Copyright Law. No part of this publication (Contents and/or Cover) may be reproduced, stored in a retrieval system or transmitted in any form by any means, electronic, mechanical, photocopy, recording or otherwise without the express written consent of the Publisher.

FIRST PRINTING 1993
SECOND PRINTING 2003
THIRD PRINTING 2010

© 2011 Jacqueline T. Flowers

All rights reserved. No part of this publication may be reproduced or transmitted in any form or by any means electronic or mechanical, including photocopy, recording, or any information storage and retrieval system, without permission in writing from both the copyright owner and the publisher.

Requests for permission to make copies of any part of this work should be mailed to Permissions Department, Llumina Christian Books, Ocala, Fl 34482.

ISBN: 978-1-62550-390-9

Printed in the United States of America by Llumina Christian Books

Table of Contents

Dedication

Undertaking additional responsibilities is not an easy task while Pastoring in the local church, preparing sermons, spending time in prayer, performing varied obligations as a wife and mother and ministering God's Word as opportunities are made available. It is because of my yearning to live in obedience to God that I am able to seize every available opportunity to bless the people of God and bring glory to the Lord Jesus Christ. I must admit, though, that the successful accomplishment of every assignment is credited to the power of God and the patient support of my husband and children. It is to them that I dedicate this work and forever thank God for their sacrifice.

It is with much love and compassion that I further dedicate this work to every member of Time of Celebration Ministries Church, Inc. and the entire Body of Christ. My prayer is that every member of the family of God will commit to deepen their individual relationship with the Lord. This book is written extensively to contribute to a more intimate relationship with the God who knows the hearts and the minds of all men. As you read *In His Presence*, I believe you will enjoy the most rewarding experience ever known and that experience is knowing and walking intimately with the God of the universe.

Hebrews 6:10
"For God is not unrighteous to forget your work and labour of love, which ye have shewed toward His name, in that ye have ministered to the saints, and do minister."

i

Foreword

As I began to write this foreword for my wife, I had to reflect on the steadfast love of God. He is identified all throughout the Bible as the "Master of Giving" from generation to generation. I praise God that I have found *"a good thing in my wife"* and obtained favor of the Lord. She is valued in our home not only as God's gift to me and our children, but as God's gift to the Body of Christ. Living with her daily affords me the opportunity to observe her and respect her as the wonderful woman she is.

Jacqueline T. Flowers has chosen to declare God's Word with an uncompromising boldness. She makes it a point to be simple and compassionate as she shares with people from all walks of life. I observe her as she seeks God's face, and captures from His heart, His Word for this generation and generations to come. She is down to earth and unpretentious. I appreciate her determination to be transparent in order that others may see that God can take an individual just as he or she is, regardless of their background, and fashion them for His glory. My wife has a servant's heart. There have been times when attempts were made to stop the fulfillment of God's purpose for her life, yet I have seen God elevate her above every attempt time and time again.

My greatest desire is to do all I can to encourage her as she hears from God so that others can reap the benefits God has prepared for all who receive Jesus Christ as Savior and Lord. As you read this book, what God has put in her will inspire you, even as it inspires me to demand excellence of myself and strive to be the best I can be in God. You will sense the Spirit of God ministering directly to you concerning your individual relationship with the Lord. Just how well do you really know the God you sing about, talk about, or preach about? I pray that as members of the Body of Christ read this book, they will make a fresh commitment to develop their relationship with the Lord. I have found that deepening one's relationship with God always brings conception, and after conception there's the birthing of that God-indwelt vision for your life.

My wife's first book, **"WOMAN BE WHOLE,"** inspired me to produce our first cassette album. This book has inspired me to hunger for God and His plan for my life as never before. God is speaking in these in-times and each time He speaks directly to you, He will inspire you to do something. He inspires you to act on what He has already placed within you. Abiding in the presence of God will give direction to your life and cause you to experience a walk with the Father that you never imagined possible.

I want to say to my wife, I love you and I am grateful to God for all that He inspires you to do. I commit to always support you in every endeavor. I know what God has planned for our lives will bring Him glory, edify the Body of Christ, and be a continual source of fulfillment.

Jerry W. Flowers, Sr.

Chapter One

We Must Pray

*I*n this dispensation of grace, much needs to be said concerning man's relationship with God. Many have received Jesus as Savior but have neglected the daily development of genuine fellowship with God as our Heavenly Father. Many have been told God is the Healer, the Keeper, and the Provider. Yet, they have not experienced Him as the Healer, the Keeper, the Provider, the Deliverer or all that He reveals Himself to be in His Word. Believers today, must come to the realization that even though God has vowed to heal, provide, grant answers to prayers and, yes, even fulfill the desires of the heart, there is still so much more God has for His children. It is sad to see that so many know about God but are not intimately acquainted with God through a personal relationship, and regular fellowship. A person can be saved and yet, forfeit the benefits of salvation if they are not taught to develop their relationship and fellowship with God.

God desires for His people to relate to Him because of who He is. He does not want to be viewed as just someone to be called upon in an emergency or out of sheer desperation. Yet we clearly understand it is a believer's covenant right to call upon the Lord in days of trouble, fully assured that God will not only hear, but answer as well. God simply wants us to love Him more than the benefits He provides. He wants to be looked upon as so much more than a mere "charge account" or a "Cosmic Santa Claus." God wants our faith to rest in who He is, not in what He does or does not do for us. He wants us to fellowship with Him because we love Him.

Contrary to what many believe, prayer is more than believing and receiving. It is more than man's need crying out to God for help. It is <u>more</u> than a time for man to vent his anger and frustrations. God is never to be looked upon as a mere sounding board. Prayer is communion (this is better explained in Chapter 5). True fellowship with God, from the heart, affords man the opportunity to know his Maker and gives his Maker an opportunity to not only speak to him, but reveal Himself and His ways to His children. The word "know" signifies more than a casual acquaintance, but rather refers to a deep, intimate relationship, wherein man literally learns the ways of God and conforms to those ways. Prayer gives man an opportunity to be still before God, allowing God to be more than a listener, but also one who speaks to the heart of man, giving protection, instruction and direction. Our time of fellowship with the Father is not to be viewed as a "gimme-gimme" line, where believers are full of wants and requests, yet void of true relationship. Prayer is a time of reflecting, repentance and refreshing. **Prayer releases power**.

God wants His Body to reach a point where there is no lack because of acquaintance with the One who not only owns "the cattle on a thousand hills," but the hills as well. When we genuinely know God as our Father and walk with Him, there will be no need He does not satisfy abundantly. This is why God says in **Matthew 6:33,** *"But seek ye first the kingdom of God, and his righteousness; and <u>all these things</u> shall be added unto you."* God desires relationship. He desires oneness. He desires fellowship. Man's relationship with God must be prized above the tangibles and the intangibles. This experience will not occur without relationship and fellowship. Relationship and fellowship cannot happen apart from His Presence. God's people can genuinely come to know Him as Father.

In these last days, God is calling for a people who are willing to live *In His Presence*. Being in the presence of God does not make believers spooky, nor does it cause believers to appear weird. Being in God's presence brings refreshing. It causes thirsts to cease and hungry souls to be satisfied. This is why the Bible says in **Psalm 34:8,** *"O taste and see that the Lord is good: blessed is the man that trusteth in Him."* Taste refers to experience. Deliverance can be experienced. Healing can be experienced. Fulfillment and inner peace can be experienced. What benefits we can enjoy as a result of living in the presence of God! To live in God's presence is a privilege and honor. This is God's invitation to His children to dine sumptuously at His royal table and be filled.

God is not some "mystical being" way off in the great outer-space. He is not some creature foreign to life and untouchable when it comes to the challenges of life. Many are seeking direction for their lives, healing for their diseased bodies, and peace for their troubled and enslaved souls. God has always possessed the answer. How can we draw wisdom for life today independent of His presence? This book reveals the key to walking in God's perfect will for life on a consistent day to day basis. It further reveals how man can clearly know the will of God for his life. No believer has to wander aimlessly through life lacking fulfillment, purpose and insight. Every child of God can have comprehensive insight into the ways and purposes of God as he or she commits to abide in the Father's Presence. The Spirit of God spoke to me in prayer, saying, *"The answers to life's challenges will not come for those who refuse to spend time in My presence.* " Time in God's presence is simply the time we spend fellowshipping and communing with Him as our heavenly Father. Success in life, ministry, and so much more will not happen apart from His Presence. Perhaps you have been seeking God for financial wholeness, success in ministry, relationships, etc. Whatever your particular situation, let me encourage you to position yourself in a place of prayer. I speak not of the physical posture of the body. I speak of the position of the heart. Prayer is more than one or two hours spent making faith affirmations. Prayer is living in the presence of God. It is being in place where you are ever conscious of the Father's presence, discerning His voice and following His instructions. It is consistent communion and fellowship with the God of the Universe. No decision is made without Him. Impossible? Nothing is impossible with God and you can know Him so intimately that every part of your being is yielded to Him.

This book does not deal with the various types of prayer. There are many authors who pride themselves on their in-depth studies and books referring to the many types of prayer. This book inspires the reader to develop an intimate relationship with the God of the Universe by spending time with Him through consistent, disciplined fellowship, communion and study of God's Word. Many have thought it impossible to know God. It was while teaching a class on "Intimacy with God", that the Spirit of God spoke these words to me, *"Intimacy with God cannot be taught, it must be experienced and many will not experience intimacy with Me in the dimension I desire, because they are not willing to pay the price."* God said, *"You can direct and instruct the people according to My Word, the Bible, but they must know intimacy through experience."* After hearing God's

4

words immediately I asked, "What is the price?" The price is a life so yielded to God that He can function in and through that life at any given time in any way He chooses. The price is total obedience. Intimacy with God, cannot be taught, it must be experienced.

Perhaps you have questions about yieldedness before God. You will find out more about it in this book. For those who are willing to pay the price, brace yourself for the most explicitly rewarding experience of your life. Our God is knowable, and yes, He is actively involved in the affairs of men. This book, "*In His Presence*", will stir up a hunger in you for the presence of God and direct you as you develop your relationship with God, who is everlastingly faithful, Amen. Take your time as you find out how every area of your life can be saturated with the presence of God. The journey is fulfilling to the one who prays, and beneficial to all those who come to know us.

The Desire of God's Heart

*T*he Bible reveals, in the book of Genesis, that God had a wonderful desire. It is in the Bible that God unfolds His ultimate desire in creation. God desired to have a relationship with someone exactly like Himself. He wanted to fellowship with someone who had a free-will to choose. He did not want a clone, robot, or someone He had to force to love and worship Him. God desired a relationship with one who would willingly and freely choose to love Him. Why was this desire so paramount? This is easy to understand when we consider that the very essence of God's nature is love.

I John 4:16
And we have known and believed the love that God hath to us. God is love; and he that dwelleth in love dwelleth in God, and God in him.

The God of the universe is love. He longed to experience love of this same caliber from one like unto Himself; someone with His nature. God could not have fellowship with anyone who possessed a nature inferior in holiness to His own. He desired a perfectly holy, free, moral agent exactly like Himself, with whom He could walk and talk.

It is in **Genesis 1:25** that God reveals His plan to the Godhead. The Godhead, often referred to as the Trinity, is God the Father, Jesus the Son, and the Holy Spirit who is the power of God. The Holy Spirit executes the plan of God by giving life to whatever God speaks. God speaks the Word and Jesus is the Word, upholding all that God speaks. The following scriptures reveal and confirm that Jesus is the Word made flesh. The Holy Spirit empowers the Word and Jesus upholds all things by the Word of His Power:

Isaiah 55:11

So shall my word be that goeth forth out of my mouth: it shall not return unto me void, but it shall accomplish that which I please, and it shall prosper in the thing whereunto I sent it.

John 1:1

In the beginning was the Word, and the Word was with God, and the Word was God.

John 1:14

And the Word was made flesh, and dwelt among us, and we beheld His glory, the glory as of the only begotten of the Father, full of grace and truth.

Hebrews 1:1-3

God, who at sundry times and in divers manners spake in time past unto the fathers by the prophets, hath in these last days spoken unto us by His Son, whom he hath appointed heir of all things, by whom also he made the worlds; who being the brightness of His glory, and the express image of His

*person, and upholding all things by the Word
of His power, when He had by Himself purged
our sins, sat down on the right hand of the
Majesty on high;...*

John 6:63
*It is the spirit that quickeneth; the flesh
profiteth nothing: the words that I speak unto
you, they are spirit, and they are life.*

II Corinthians 3:6
*Who also hath made us able ministers of the
new testament; not of the letter, but of the
Spirit: for the letter killeth, but the Spirit
giveth life.*

Further, God unveils His plan to the Holy Spirit and
Jesus saying...

Genesis 1:25-28
*Let us make man in our image, after our
likeness: and let them have dominion over
the fish of the sea and over the fowl of the air,
and over the cattle, and over all the earth,
and over every creeping thing that creepeth
upon the earth. So God created man in His
own image, in the image of God created he
him; male and female created he them. And
God blessed them, and God said unto them,
be fruitful and multiply and replenish the
earth, and subdue it: and have dominion over
the fish of the sea and over the fowl of the air,
and over every living thing that moveth upon
the earth.*

These verses reveal the initial plan of God for family. God revealed that He would create man. In the above verses He speaks generically, referring to male and female or the species of mankind. He said He would create man in His own image after His own likeness. Man would be an exact duplicate of God. After God reveals His plan, He establishes the fact that man is to be fashioned as a ruler like unto Himself. Man, referring to the species of mankind, would have dominion over planet earth and live life eternally, in a blessed state, reigning over all God created, walking and talking with the Creator of the ends of the earth. What an awesome plan!

I am certain as God speaks, Jesus says, *"I'll uphold what you speak"* and the Holy Spirit says *"I'll give life to what you speak."* God the Father sets out to implement what was already within Him. For it is within the depths of God that the plan for every person who would ever walk planet earth existed. Let us just consider how God caused what was already evident within Him to become a visible reality.

Genesis 2:7-8
And the Lord God formed man of the dust of the ground, and breathed into his nostrils the breath of life; and man became a living soul. And the Lord God planted a garden eastward in Eden; and there He put the man whom He had formed.

Only an awesomely powerful and all-knowing God could take the dust of the ground and from dust fashion and form a physical body to house a literal spirit. Before God ever created man, He fashioned the world which He predestined man to rule. He literally fashioned the dirt that He intended to use to compose the anatomy of the physical body. God designed from dust the skeletal system. The word "skeleton" was derived from a word which means a dried up body. This framework God designed is comprised of two hundred and six (206) bones. Eighty (80) axial or trunk bones, one hundred twenty-six (26) limb bones not including the teeth. He gave the veins, arteries, organs, nerves, glands, blood, skin, tissue, cells, capillaries, muscles and so much more to organize the various functions of the body. God designed what we know today as the circulatory, digestive, muscular, nervous, reproductive, skeletal and respiratory systems all for one distinct purpose. He chose to house the spirit in a facility that could respond properly to, function in and readily adapt to the natural order of creation itself. God knew He would then have an exquisite habitation for the life-force which is the spirit.

The physical body, though an exquisite masterpiece and excellent example of workmanship, was void of life. It was then that God breathed into the nostrils of this masterpiece the breath of life. Where did this breath of life come from? This breath of life was the life within God entering the dried up physical body. God literally released from within Himself, His life, His nature, His person into this body, and man became a living soul.

Genesis 2:7-9
And the Lord God formed man of the dust of the ground, and breathed into his nostrils the breath of life; and man became a living soul. And the Lord God planted a garden eastward in Eden; and there he put the man whom he had formed. And out of the ground made the

*Lord God to grow every tree that is pleasant
to the sight, and good for food; the tree of life
also in the midst of the garden, and the tree of
knowledge of good and evil.*

God took the actual life force (the spirit) for which He
fashioned a physical body and gave him a soul. God gave
man the ability to choose, to reason, to express emotions,
feel and imagine. What was once a desire, a plan in the
mind of God, was now becoming a reality. This reality still
had many other components to fall into place, but before
developing these components God gave Adam some specific
instructions to follow.

Genesis 2:15-20

*And the Lord God took the man, and put
him into the garden of Eden to dress it and
to keep it. And the Lord God commanded
the man, saying, of every tree of the garden
thou mayest freely eat: but of the tree of the
knowledge of good and evil, thou shalt not
eat of it: for in the day that thou eatest thereof
thou shalt surely die. And the Lord God said,
it is not good that the man should be alone;
I will make him an help meet for him. And
out of the ground the Lord God formed every
beast of the field, and every fowl of the air;
and brought them unto Adam to see what
he would call them: and whatsoever Adam
called every living creature, that was the
name thereof. And Adam gave names to all
cattle, and to the fowl of the air, and to every
beast of the field; but for Adam there was not
found an help meet for him.*

Can you imagine the time it must have taken for Adam to literally name the fowl of the air, the cattle and every creeping thing that crept upon the earth? It seems appropriate to conclude that Adam had been delegated a task that required a great deal of time and attention. However, we must understand that we have no way to determine how long it took Adam to complete such a task. The Bible says in **II Peter 3:8;** *"But, beloved, be not ignorant of this one thing, that one day is with the Lord as a thousand years, and a thousand years as one day."* **Psalm 90:4;** *"For a thousand years in thy sight are but as yesterday when it is past, and as a watch in the night."*

Upon completion of Adam's assignment, the Bible records that something was missing. There was no one suitable for Adam and adaptable to him. This was apparent because God forestated in **Genesis 2:27** that He would create male and female in His image and bless them and allow them to have dominion. Therefore, He could do no less.

In order to comprehend this clearly let us go back to **Genesis 3:27**. In the original Hebrew, **Genesis 3:27** *reads,* *"God created the man and the woman exact duplicates of Himself."* God is Spirit and since we understand that spirit-life comes from God, we must further understand that within God abides the male and female life-force or spirit life. Therefore God is masculine and feminine in Spirit. Spirit-life is in God and comes from God, for not only is God Spirit, but He is the Father of spirits. God is the originator of life. In **Exodus 3:14** God refers to Himself as **"I AM THAT I AM."** **I AM** in the Hebrew means self-existing, or uncaused. Self existence simply means life within one's self. God has no origin, yet He is the origin of all He creates. **John 4:24** affirms the fact that God is Spirit. Even as God is Spirit, man is spirit, however God fashioned a physical body to house man's spirit and gave man a soul. This was done so that man could function adequately on planet earth.

John 5:26
For as the Father has life in Himself, so He has granted the Son to have life in Himself.

Hebrews 12:9
...shall we not much rather be in subjection unto the Father of spirits, and live?

I Thessalonians 5:23
And the very God of peace sanctify you wholly; and I pray God your whole spirit and soul and body be preserved blameless unto the coming of our Lord Jesus Christ.

Acts 17:24-28
God that made the world and all things therein, seeing that he is Lord of heaven and earth, dwelleth not in temples made with hands; neither is worshipped with men's hands, as though he needed any thing, seeing he giveth to all life, and breath and all things; and hath made of one blood all nations of men for to dwell on all the face of the earth, and hath determined the times before appointed, and the bounds of their habitation; that they should seek the Lord if haply they might feel after him, and find him, though he be not far from every one of us: for in him we live, and move, and have our being; as certain also of your own poets have said, for we are also His offspring.

Before God fashioned Adam's body, Adam's spirit was with God. When God fashioned Adam's physical body He breathed the spirit-life, male and female into Adam. Then God extracted the female from the male and skillfully hand-crafted someone suitable and adaptable to man, called "WOMAN." We understand this clearly when we consider that the original Hebrew for woman is **"Ish-shah."** Ish-shah literally means she-man, womb-man; man with the womb; or female man. Woman represents the female aspect of God's Spirit.

Genesis 2:21-23
And the Lord God caused a deep sleep to fall upon Adam, and he slept: and he took one of his ribs, and closed up the flesh instead thereof; and the rib, which the Lord God had taken from man, made he a woman and brought her unto the man. And Adam said, this is now bone of my bones, and flesh of my flesh: she shall be called Woman, because she was taken out of Man.

God took the rib, which in the original Hebrew means side, and extracted the female side of Himself. It is from the side or rib of Adam that God fashioned someone equal to man, called woman. The distinct difference existed only in the design of the female's body. God fashioned certain facets of a woman's body in order for man to specifically recognize God did not fashion another man like unto Adam for cohabitation, but a woman. Adam and Eve were designed to rule the earth jointly as they complimented one another and drew strength from one another. Woman was designed to rule in the realm of influence, as helper, as life-giver. She responds to the needs of man. She is a nurturer. Man has a more rational disposition. He was designed in or with authority to protect the woman. This is better explained in my book, "***Where Are The Men?***"

God designed man to be man and woman to be woman. God did not make another man to serve as Adam's help meet or one suitable for and adaptable to Adam. By the same token we understand that God formed man first and gave woman to him. God did not make woman for woman. This is why it is an abomination before God for men to attempt to be women or women to attempt to be men. This is not God's design, neither is it acceptable in God's eyes because man and woman represent the glory and presence of God in the earth. The following scriptures are clear on God's views concerning His plan for mankind:

Genesis 3:24-25
Therefore shall a man leave his father and his mother, and shall cleave unto his wife: and they shall be one flesh. And they were both naked, the man and his wife, and were not ashamed.

Romans 1:26-32
For this cause God gave them up unto vile affections: for even their women did change the natural use into that which is against nature: And likewise also the men, leaving the natural use of the woman, burned in their lust one toward another; men with men working that which is unseemly, and receiving in themselves that recompense of their error which was meet. And even as they did not like to retain God in their knowledge, God

*gave them over to a reprobate mind, to do
those things which are not convenient; being
filled with all unrighteousness, fornication,
wickedness, covetousness, maliciousness;
full of envy, murder, debate, deceit,
malignity; whisperers, backbiters, haters of
God, despiteful, proud, boasters, inventors
of evil things, disobedient to parents, without
understanding, covenant breakers, without
natural affection, implacable, unmerciful:
who knowing the judgment of God, that they
which commit such things are worthy of
death, not only do the same, but have pleasure
in them that do them.*

Leviticus 18:22
*Thou shalt not lie with mankind, as with
womankind: it is abomination.*

God's perfect and pure plan is that all the earth be filled
with His glory. He fashioned male and female exactly like
unto Himself for relationship and fellowship. He provides
all that is necessary for fulfillment in life. He clothes the
male and female with His glory and honor, and places
them over the works of His hands. He established adequate
representation of Himself in the earth.

Psalm 8:1-6
*O Lord our Lord, how excellent is thy name
in all the earth! Who hast set thy glory above
the heavens. Out of the mouth of babes and
sucklings hast thou ordained strength because
of thine enemies, that thou mightest still the
enemy and the avenger. When I consider thy*

*heavens, the work of thy fingers, the moon
and the stars, which thou ordained; What is
man, that thou art mindful of him? and the
son of man, that thou visitest him? For thou
hast made him a little lower than the angels,
and hast crowned him with glory and honor.
Thou madest him to have dominion over the
works of thy hands; thou hast put all things
under His feet.*

The word angels in the above verses comes from the original Hebrew word **"Elohim"** which means Gods, referring to God the Father, God the Son and God the Holy Ghost. The Psalmist records that God made man a little lower than Himself.

That which existed first within God was now a reality. Man and woman, male and female, created in the image and likeness of God, available to love God with the same caliber of love by which God loved them, and the freedom to love each other unconditionally. Adam and Eve were free moral agents, able to express emotion and represent God in the earth by exemplifying rulership and stewardship over the works of the Father's hands. God was pleased as He reflected on all He had created and said *"IT WAS VERY GOOD."*

Genesis 2:28-31
*And God blessed them, and God said unto
them, be fruitful, and multiply, and replenish
the earth, and subdue it: and have dominion
over the fish of the sea, and over the fowl of
the air, and over every living thing that moveth
upon the earth. And God said, behold, I have
given you every herb bearing seed, which is*

upon the face of all the earth, and every tree,
in the which is the fruit of a tree yielding seed;
to you it shall be for meat. And to every beast
of the earth, and to every fowl of the air, and
to every thing that creepeth upon the earth,
wherein there is life, I have given every green
herb for meat: and it was so. And God saw
every thing that he had made, and, behold, IT
WAS VERY GOOD....

Yes, God created mankind to fellowship with Him; to represent Him in the earth; and exercise wise stewardship of all the works of God's hands.

Chapter Three

Forfeiting the Presence of God

*A*fter creating Adam and Eve, there was only one thing God required, obedience. God gives Adam and Eve liberty to enjoy life to its fullest, and only required that they follow His instructions. It is important to understand that God gave Adam certain instructions before He ever physically created the woman. Let me re-emphasize that God ultimately designed man to protect the woman while carrying out the Father's instructions to the letter.

Genesis 2:17
But of the tree of the knowledge of good and evil, thou shalt not eat of it: for in the day that thou eatest thereof thou shalt surely die.

God told Adam if he disobeyed, he would die. What did this mean? Would God kill Adam if he disobeyed? God was speaking of a spiritual death, a spiritual separation. Adam would immediately be stripped of the glory of God and lose the nature of God. He would no longer be God-indwelt, neither would he be a ruler. But, he would become a slave to sin and a child of the devil. Man would no longer have direct fellowship with God, for his nature would alienate him from the Father. Adam would be dead to God and alive to evil. His nature would be immediately transformed from the nature of God to the nature of satan. He would become mentally unorganized and set in motion the aging process which would lead to physical death.

Ultimately Adam and Eve were authorized to keep order in this earth by following God's instructions, embracing the Word of God and refusing at all costs to violate God's distinct instructions. God warned them of the penalty for disobedience.

Adam and Eve were blessed by God and all nations of the earth would come forth from them. The earth would be replenished and what was once a desire in the heart of God would be a reality in the earth. God told them to be productive; contribute to the productivity of others and leave a deposit in the earth for future generations.

A relationship with God is built upon respect for God's Word and is demonstrated by obedience, communication, fellowship with God and trust in God. If any relationship is to remain strong, there must be respect, communication, and trust. God communicated with Adam and Eve daily. He trusted them and He respected their right to choose. God knew that any relationship void of these elements <u>would be</u> thrown into literal chaos and <u>would not</u> last. It is important that we pay careful attention to the next scripture, for in these verses we see the entire human race plunged into chaos:

Genesis 3:1-11

Now the serpent was more subtle than any beast of the field which the Lord God had made. And he said unto the woman, yea, hath God said, ye shall not eat of every tree of the garden? And the woman said unto the serpent, we may eat of the fruit of the trees of the garden: but of the fruit of the tree which is in the midst of the garden, God hath said, ye shall not eat of it, neither shall ye touch it, lest ye die. And the serpent said unto the woman, ye shall not surely die: for God doth know that in the day ye eat thereof, then your eyes shall be opened, and ye shall be as gods, knowing good and evil. And when the woman saw that the tree was good for food, and that it was pleasant to the eyes, and a tree to be desired to make one wise, she took of the fruit there of, and did eat, and gave also unto her husband with her; and he did eat. And the eyes of them both were opened, and they knew that they were naked; and they sewed fig leaves together, and made themselves aprons. And they heard the voice of the Lord God walking in the garden in the cool of the day: and Adam and his wife hid themselves from the presence of the Lord God amongst the trees of the garden. And the Lord God called unto Adam, and said unto him, Where art thou? And he said, I heard thy voice in the garden, and I was afraid, because I was naked and I hid myself. And He said, who told thee that thou was naked? Hast thou eaten of the tree, whereof I commanded thee that thou shouldest not eat?

The time span between when God formed Adam and Eve up to **Genesis 3:1-11** is not revealed. Therefore, it is possible that they had been in the garden several hundreds of years before **Genesis chapter 3**. Why? Because they were not aging. They were not created to die. Adam and Eve were not created to experience physical death. They were created to live eternally. However, let's see how the process of physical death began as we explore several things happening in the above verses. First we see the devil approaches Eve in the form of a serpent. He begins to question the validity of God's Word. He uses the same strategy today. He comes to bring doubt to the Christian's mind. Whenever there is a question about the validity of God's Word, the Christian should stop and consider carefully what God's Word says and refuse to entertain any thoughts questioning or opposing the Word of God.

Numbers 23:19

God is not a man, that he should lie; neither the son of man, that he should repent: hath he said, and shall he not do it? Or hath he spoken, and shall he not make it good?

Matthew 24:35

Heaven and earth shall pass away, but my words shall not pass away.

Psalm 119:89

For ever, O Lord, thy word is settled in heaven.

Satan <u>feeds</u> Eve with information contradictory to what God said. God specifically said, *"Do not eat of the fruit of the tree in the midst of the garden."* God meant exactly what He said. He allowed Adam and Eve leisure and liberty throughout the entire garden of Eden. Why was Eve so enticed by this particular tree and its fruit? Adam had clearly conveyed God's instructions to Eve, *"...in the day that thou eatest thereof thou shalt surely die."* The devil knew the power of influence that had been delegated to Eve. He, being the master of deception, distracted her by causing her to focus on the fruit and doubt the truth of God. His shear aim was to entice her to disobey God and, thereby, encourage Adam, her husband, to rebel against God. Eve <u>attempts</u> to explain what God has said. Man need never explain his position of obedience to the devil, nor the integrity of God's Word to those who oppose truth. All God <u>requires</u> is that His children obey His voice. He will always honor His Word. Eve listen to the voice of satan and <u>yielded</u> to the temptation. She then <u>influenced</u> Adam to partake in her willful disobedience of God's Word. The devil will always use us to influence or coerce others to violate the mandates of God.

Why was satan so interested in enticing Eve to sin against God? He is the spirit of error and his total objective is to get man's focus away from that which gives protection, direction, and purpose to life. As long as man keeps his eyes on God he will dwell in safety. Before Adam and Eve disobeyed God, their physical eyes were already opened. How else could they have seen the fruit or even one another? The devil tells Eve her eyes would be opened if she ate of the fruit. He knew Adam and Eve were innocent and had no awareness of sin or evil. When the Bible says their eyes were opened, it refers to awareness or enlightenment. After Adam and Eve disobeyed God, their eyes were opened to sin, the awareness of evil. They had no prior knowledge or awareness of sin--evil, for they walked in the fullness of holy illumination, the light of God. The moment they disobeyed:

- they were stripped of the Glory of God and forfeited His presence, His nature, His life;
- they were separated from their Maker spiritually; they became void of the glory of God;
- they experienced embarrassment, condemnation, shame, guilt, fear, and spiritual death, which is separation

from God. The experience of fear, guilt, embarrassment, condemnation and shame were feelings and emotions Adam and Eve had never known before.

They were accustomed to being arrayed with the glory of God, the fact that they were physically naked only became apparent to emphasize man's depraved state; the guilt and shame, that is a direct result of a life void of the presence of God. Adam and Eve now knew the emptiness of lost union with a Holy and Just God. They had no life, no protection and their nakedness revealed their fallen state. The process of physical death began. The aging process began. Man became subject to sickness and diseases. Physical death is a separation of the spirit and soul from the physical body. The spirit-life, the real individual either goes to heaven or hell (based upon acceptance or rejection of the Lord Jesus Christ) and the earth-suit or physical body goes back to dust.

Satan deceived Eve into thinking she could become more like God than she already was. Man must always see Himself as God sees him and this reflection can only be seen in the Word of God. Eve had God's Word from the beginning; for He created her and Adam in His image, after His likeness.

Psalm 82:6
I have said, Ye are gods; and all of you are children of the most High.

John 10:34-38
Jesus answered them, is it not written in your law, I said, ye are gods? If he called them gods, unto whom the word of God came, and the scripture cannot be broken; say ye of him, whom the Father hath sanctified, and sent

into the world, thou blasphemest; because I said, I am the Son of God? If I do not the works of my Father, believe me not. But if I do, though ye believe not me, believe the works: that ye may know, and believe, that the Father is in me, and I in him.

As we have already verified by scripture, God fashioned Adam and Eve just a little lower than Himself and crowned them with glory and honor. He placed them over the works of His hands. Satan is God's enemy and was observing all God was doing. His name was Lucifer before he was identified as the devil. There was a time when Lucifer ruled in perfection and sinlessness before God ever fashioned Adam. Lucifer was once an angel in Heaven. He was called the anointed cherub. The Bible records that one day he decided he would rebel against God and exalt himself above God. As a result, he was cast out of heaven along with one-third of the angels he deceived into conspiring with him against God. When he and his cohorts were cast out, they brought utter desolation to planet earth. They became dis-embodied or demon spirits. From that time to this day, they have endeavored to war against God even though they know they are defeated and hell awaits them. Hell was prepared for satan and his cohorts, not mankind. Man is God's representative in planet earth. The devil cannot destroy God. He is no match for God, so he seeks to destroy God's image, men and women who are born-again.

The devil hates the presence of God in the earth. He looked for a way to gain rulership in this earth after his dethroning. He devised a plan that would literally plunge all mankind into chaos if he could convince (persuade) Adam and Eve to listen and violate God's Word.

In **Genesis chapter 3**, satan enters as a serpent, as we have seen. The serpent was not satan. Satan used the serpent. Satan is a dis-embodied spirit, a fallen angel. He simply used the serpent as a channel to deceive Eve. He endeavored to take advantage of her, fully aware that the success of his plan was dependent on the woman influencing the man to disobey God. Lucifer and the angels that fell with him are sly and cunning. They get their widest range of expression through mankind. If they cannot live in a human body, they will use animals, reptiles, etc. Since Adam and Eve had the nature of God, the devil could not inhabit them, but he could make attempts to deceive and manipulate.

Isaiah 14:12-17

How art thou fallen from heaven, O Lucifer, son of the morning! How art thou cut down to the ground, which didst weaken the nations! For thou hast said in thine heart, I will ascend into heaven, I will exalt my throne above the stars of God: I will sit also upon the mount of the congregation, in the sides of the north: I will ascend above the heights of the clouds; I will be like the most High. Yet thou shalt be brought down to hell, to the sides of the pit. They that see thee shall narrowly look upon thee, and consider thee, saying, Is this the man that made the earth to tremble, that did shake kingdoms; that made the world as a wilderness, and destroyed the cities thereof; that opened not the house of his prisoners?

Ezekiel 28:11-19

Moreover the word of the Lord came unto me, saying, Son of man, take up a lamentation upon the king of Tyrus, and say unto him, thus saith the Lord God; thou sealest up the sum, full of wisdom, and perfect in beauty. Thou hast been in Eden the garden of God; every precious stone was thy covering, the sardius, topaz and the diamond, the beryl, the onyx, and the jasper, the sapphire, the emerald, and the carbuncle, and gold: the workmanship of thy tabrets and of thy pipes was prepared in thee in the day that thou wast created, till iniquity was found in thee. By the multitude of thy merchandise they have filled the midst of thee with violence, and thou hast sinned: therefore I will cast thee as profane out of the mountain of God: and I will destroy thee, O covering cherub, from the midst of the stones of fire. Thine heart was lifted up because of thy beauty, thou hast corrupted thy wisdom by reason of thy brightness: I will cast thee to the ground, I will lay thee before kings, that they may behold thee. Thou hast defiled thy sanctuaries by the multitude of thine iniquities, by the iniquity of thy traffic; therefore will I bring forth a fire from the midst of thee, it shall devour thee, and I will bring thee to ashes upon the earth in the sight of all them that behold thee. All they that know thee among the people shall be astonished at thee: thou shalt be a terror, and never shalt thou be any more.

Revelation 12:7-12

And there was war in heaven: Michael and his angels fought against the dragon; and the

29

> *dragon fought and his angels and prevailed*
> *not; neither was their place found any*
> *more in heaven. And the great dragon was*
> *cast out, that old serpent, called the devil,*
> *and Satan, which deceiveth the whole*
> *world: he was cast out into the earth, and*
> *his angels were cast out with him. And I*
> *heard a loud voice saying in heaven, now*
> *is come salvation, and strength, and the*
> *Kingdom of our God, and the power of His*
> *Christ: for the accuser of our brethren is*
> *cast down, which accused them before our*
> *God day and night. And they overcame him*
> *by the blood of the Lamb, and by the Word*
> *of their testimony; and they loved not their*
> *lives unto the death. Therefore rejoice, ye*
> *heavens, and ye that dwell in them. Woe*
> *to the inhabitants of the earth and of the*
> *sea? For the devil is come down unto you,*
> *having great wrath, because he knoweth*
> *that he hast but a short time.*

The devil deceived Eve by telling her she would become like God if she ate the fruit. How could Adam and Eve become any more like God than they already were; as clearly seen in scripture? Eve failed to see herself as the exact image of God. I will reiterate the fact that Adam and Eve only had the awareness of good. **They had not known sin**. They had not known separation from God. They represented the presence of God in the earth and this, the devil hated. He hated the relationship and fellowship Adam and Eve had with God. He despised the fact that they were clothed with the glory of God. He hated the innocence, the holiness and the fact that they ruled planet earth.

After Adam and Eve sinned, they tried to hide themselves from the presence of God. The guilt of sin will always cause a man to flee from the presence of God. Yet, it's amazing that God invites us to come into His presence, even when we miss it and sin. Let's look carefully at the following verses.

Genesis 3:8-13

And they heard the voice of the Lord God walking in the garden in the cool of the day: and Adam and his wife hid themselves from the presence of the Lord God amongst the trees of the garden. And the Lord God called unto Adam, and said unto him, where art thou? And he said I heard thy voice in the garden, and I was afraid, because I was naked; and I hid myself. And he said, who told thee that thou wast naked? Hast thou eaten of the tree, whereof I commanded thee that thou shouldest not eat? And the man said, the woman whom thou gavest to be with me, she gave me of the tree, and I did eat. And the Lord God said unto the woman, what is this that thou hast done? And the woman said, the serpent beguiled me, and I did eat.

When God looked for Adam and Eve, He knew where they were geographically. But, He was acknowledging that their spiritual position as children of God, rulers in the earth, was vacant. He saw that they no longer sat in the seat of spiritual holiness, authority and rulership. Satan now had rulership over the earth. When God said, *"Where art thou?"*, He was saying in essence, *"Adam, do you know what you have done?"* He was making reference to the broken union and fellowship Adam and Eve once had with

31

Him. They were now children of the devil and their rightful position as children of God had been severed. The accusation of who was at fault was the normal result of their sinful state and the initiator of it all was laughing, for he (the devil) had achieved just what he wanted.

His ploy all along was to deceive the woman by perverting the truth of God's Word and then watch the woman coerce Adam into rebellion against God. Adam and Eve experienced separation from God and satan legally gained entrance into the earth, as god of this world.

II Corinthians 4:3-4
But if our gospel be hid, it is hid to them that are lost: In whom the god of this world hath blinded the minds of them which believe not, lest the light of the glorious gospel of Christ, who is the image of God, should shine unto them.

The devil did not care about Adam and Eve. His war was with God. Adam and Eve represented the avenue by which satan sought to gain authority over all the earth and the entire human race. His strategy was successful. Adam and Eve sinned against God and as a result, all mankind partook of their sin and its universal effect. Adam and Eve's decision to violate God's divine order caused chaos in the earth. Their decision brought spiritual death, the process of physical death, poverty, sickness, pain, sorrow, misery, condemnation and so much more upon all mankind. Man's plight in life would be filled with self-gratification, lusts, dead-end habits, hardships, unbelief, and unkindness in every form without God. All mankind became blind to kingdom realities, defiled in conscience, obstinate, and rebellious.

Romans 5:12

Wherefore, as by one man sin entered into the world, and death by sin; and so death passed upon all men, for that all have sinned:

Man was created by God for relationship and fellowship with God. Without the presence of God, man's heart cries out in anguish. Man innately yearns for fulfillment through communion with His Maker. Initially Adam and Eve had perfect union with God. Every part of their lives had been saturated with the love and the glory of God. However, satan would stop at nothing to destroy the image of God in the earth, and yes even today, though a defeated foe, (one who will not prevail) satan will stop at nothing as he attempts to destroy the Body of Christ, the image of God in this earth.

John 10:10

The thief cometh not, but for to steal, and to kill, and to destroy... ...

Rulership Re-established

*A*ll mankind originated from Adam and Eve and thus, the sinfulness of Adam and Eve passed upon the entire human race. Spiritual death is inherited at the conception of every person born in this world. Every person enters this earth void of the life and nature of God. Adam and Eve's violation of God's Word caused every man and woman to inherit the nature of satan. Mankind is separated from God, not because of what he has done, but because the sin nature he inherited separates him from God. The penalty of transgression passed upon the entire species of mankind because every person born into planet earth is a partaker of Adam and Eve's sin, not by similitude but inheritance, and subject to the consequences of that sin.

Psalm 51:1-5

Have mercy upon me, O God, according to Thy lovingkindness: according unto the multitude of Thy tender mercies blot out my transgressions. Wash me throughly from mine iniquity, and cleanse me from my sin. I acknowledge my transgressions: and my sin is ever before me. Against Thee, Thee only, have I sinned, and done this evil in Thy sight: that Thou mightest be justified when Thou speakest, and be clear when Thou Judgest. Behold, I was shapen in iniquity; and in sin did my mother conceive me.

Romans 3:23

For all have sinned, and come short of the Glory of God.

Romans 3:10

As it is written, there is none righteous, no, not one: ...

Romans 6:23

For the wages of sin is death; but the gift of God is eternal life through Jesus Christ our Lord.

God's love for all mankind would not allow Him to turn His back on the depraved, fallen state of His children. God created man for His pleasure and as always, He had a master-plan which paved the way for mankind to be reunited with his Maker. This plan would enable man to enter God's Presence in absolute innocence, void of guilt and condemnation. We know this plan today as the plan of salvation.

John 3:16-17

For God so loved the world, that He gave His only begotten Son, that whosoever believeth in Him should not perish, but have everlasting life. For God sent not His Son into the world to condemn the world; but that the world through Him might be saved.

Romans 10: 9-13

That if thou shalt confess with thy mouth the Lord Jesus, and shalt believe in thine heart that God hath raised Him from the dead, thou shalt be saved. For with the heart man believeth unto righteousness; and with the mouth confession is made unto salvation. For the scripture saith, Whosoever believeth on Him shall not be ashamed. For there is no difference between the Jew and the Greek: for the same Lord over all is rich unto all that call upon Him. For whosoever shall call upon the name of the Lord shall be saved.

Ephesians 2:6-8
And hath raised us up together, and made us sit together in heavenly places in Christ Jesus: That in the ages to come He might shew the exceeding riches of His grace in His kindness toward us through Christ Jesus. For by grace are ye saved through faith; and that not of yourselves: it is the gift of God.

God does not look for ways to punish or condemn His creation. He establishes a plan by which all can be reconciled to Him.

Colossians 1:20-22
And, having made peace through the blood of His cross, by Him to reconcile all things unto Himself; by Him, I say, whether they be things in earth, or things in heaven. And you, that were sometime alienated and enemies in your mind by wicked works, yet now hath He reconciled in the body of His flesh through death, to present you holy and unblameable and unreproveable in His sight:

The above scriptures reveal the condition of man once we experience salvation. After salvation God sees us as holy, unblameable and innocent. God does not see you as a sinner or as a wretch undone. Once a man receives Jesus as Lord and Savior of his life, God sees him as His child. God sees him as one adopted into the family by virtue of the blood of the Lord Jesus Christ.

Colossians 1:12-13

Giving thanks unto the Father, which hath made us meet to be partakers of the inheritance of the saints in light: who hath delivered us from the power of darkness and translated us into the Kingdom of His dear Son.

God so longed for fellowship with man, that He would not allow anything to hinder reconciliation. He yearns for the love of His children.

In **John 5:24** we see how the yearning in God establishes the plan by which all can experience life in God. Jesus explains that man can be literally delivered from separation or alienation from God by simply accepting the Word of God, believing that Jesus is the Son of God, and that His blood has washed away man's sinful state. Jesus says, on this premise man can experience everlasting life free from the tormenting effects of sin. Those who were once spiritually dead, will hear the word of God and as they adhere to the truth, they experience spiritual life.

John 5:24-26

Verily, verily, I say unto you, He that heareth My Word, and believeth on Him that sent

Me, hath everlasting life, and shall not come into condemnation; but is passed from death unto life. Verily, verily, I say unto you, the hour is coming, and now is, when the dead (spiritually dead) shall hear the voice of the Son of God: and they that hear shall live. For as the Father hath life in Himself; so hath he given to the Son to have life in Himself; and hath given Him authority to execute judgment also, because He is the Son of man.

God ordained the plan of salvation to free man from satan's captivity. He freed man from guilt and condemnation by allowing Jesus to pay the penalty for the sins of all mankind in His own body. Many people mentally assent to this truth but refuse to allow the free gift of salvation to rule their lives. God gives man the ability to take his rightful position as a child of God free from the guilt and shame of his former state and enjoy all the privileges originally designed for him to enjoy. Even though God extends this awesome privilege to mankind, He will not force man to partake of this benefit.

John 1:12

But as many as received him, to them gave he power to become the sons of God, even to them that believe on his name.

Salvation is God's free gift. It cannot be purchased or worked for. Jesus paid the sin debt by sacrificing Himself. No attempts made by man can acquire salvation other than through man's acceptance of what Jesus has done. Acceptance of the truth should cause repentance and then conversion. Jesus willingly paid for man's redemption with His life. The significance of the sacrifice He made for us is clearly seen at Calvary. He experienced separation from His Father for all mankind, though He had never known sin. He experienced physical death in that His spirit was separated from the physical body. In order to verify that Jesus was physically dead, in **John 19:34**, the Bible says a soldier pierced Him in the side with a sword. Blood and water came streaming from His body. The blood symbolized full redemption for the sins of all mankind past, present and future. We became partakers of Sonship by His blood, and our acceptance of Him as the Christ.

John 19:34
But one of the soldiers with a spear pierced his side, and forthwith came there out blood and water.

Ephesians 1:7
In whom we have redemption through his blood, the forgiveness of sins, according to the riches of His grace;...

Water symbolizes the cleansing experience of salvation as man is baptized into the family of God by the Holy Spirit. He is totally cleansed of all transgression. The water further symbolizes the Word. We are cleansed *by the washing of the water of the Word.*

Ephesians 1:13
In whom ye also trusted, after that ye heard the Word of Truth, the gospel of your salvation: in whom also after that ye believed, ye were sealed with that Holy Spirit of promise...

Ephesians 5:26
That He might sanctify and cleanse it with the washing of water by the Word,

John 3:1-6
There was a man of the Pharisees, named Nicodemus, a ruler of the Jews: the same came to Jesus by night, and said unto him, Rabbi, we know that thou art a teacher come from God: for no man can do these miracles that thou doest, except God be with him. Jesus answered and said unto him, verily, verily, I say unto thee, except a man be born again, he cannot see (experience) The Kingdom of God. Nicodemus saith unto Him, how can a man be born when he is old? Can he enter the second time into his mother's womb, and be born? Jesus answered, verily, verily I say unto thee, except a man be born of water (acceptance of Truth) and of the Spirit (regeneration), he cannot enter into the Kingdom of God. That which is born of the flesh is flesh; and that which is born of the Spirit is spirit.

In the above scripture, Jesus explains to a man who is a Jewish Rabbi, a member of the Sanhedrin and one of the richest men in Jerusalem, the necessity of the new birth. He simply says, *"Nicodemus, you must be born again by your acceptance of the Word of God and experience baptism into the family of God by the Holy Spirit."* Jesus, the Word, extends redemption to man by His blood. Man must believe this truth with the heart and declare this truth with the mouth. The Holy Spirit baptizes man into The Body of Christ. The Holy Spirit imparts the nature and life of God to man by recreating the nature within man. The Holy Spirit instantly transforms man on the inside. Man must conform on the outside by renewing his mind and controlling his body.

I Corinthians 12:13

For by one Spirit are we all baptized into one body, whether we be Jews or Gentiles, whether we be bond or free; and have been all made to drink into one Spirit.

John 4:13-14

Jesus answered and said unto her, whosoever drinketh of this water shall thirst again, but whosoever drinketh of the water that I shall give him shall never thirst; but the water that I shall give him shall be in him a well of water springing into everlasting life.

Ephesians 5:26-27

That he might sanctify and cleanse it with the washing of water by the word, that he might present it to himself a glorious church, not having spot, or wrinkle, or any such thing; but that it should be holy and without blemish.

An awesome revelation found in God's Word is that from the side of Adam, God fashioned woman. The finished work of the creation of male and female came forth when God closed up Adam's flesh. From the side of the Lord Jesus Christ, God revealed the finished work of redemption as blood and water came forth.

Through Adam's sin, a sentence of death, without a promise of resurrection, passed upon all men. On the other hand, by the obedience of Christ, the sentence was completely canceled and original dominion restored. One is deemed a sinner through Adam. One is deemed righteous through Christ. Jesus represents the second Adam, a quickening spirit. He represents one who restores life. He paid for man's full atonement with His death, burial, and resurrection.

I Corinthians 15:45-50

And so it is written, the first man Adam was made a living soul; the last Adam was made a quickening spirit. Howbeit that was not first which is spiritual, but that which is natural; and afterward that which is spiritual. The first man is of the earth, earthy: the second man is the Lord from heaven. As is the earthy, such are also that are earthy: and as is the heavenly, such are they also that are heavenly. And as we have borne the image of the earthy, we shall also bear the image of the heavenly. Now this I say, brethren, that flesh and blood cannot inherit the kingdom of God; neither doeth corruption inherit incorruption.

Colossians 2:14-17

Blotting out the handwriting of ordinances that was against us, which was contrary to us, and took it out of the way nailing it to his cross; and having spoiled principalities and powers, he made a shew of them openly, triumphing over them in it. Let no man therefore judge you in meat, or in drink, or in respect of an holy day, or of the new moon, or of the sabbath days which are a shadow of things to come; but the body is of Christ.

As man acknowledges the following scripture, salvation is imminent.

Romans 10:9-13

That if thou shalt confess with thy mouth the Lord Jesus and shalt believe in thine heart that God hath raised him from the dead, thou shalt be saved. For with the heart man believeth unto righteousness; and with the mouth confession is made unto salvation. For the scripture saith, whosoever believeth on him shall not be ashamed. For there is no difference between the Jew and the Greek: for the same Lord over all is rich unto all that call upon him. For whosoever shall call upon the name of the Lord shall be saved.

The criteria for salvation is two-fold. One must confess with the mouth the Lord Jesus and believe in the heart. It is the spirit that was separated from God during the fall in the garden of Eden. Therefore, it is the spirit that must be made new.

Ephesians 1:3-7

Blessed be the God and Father of our Lord Jesus Christ, who hath blessed us with all spiritual blessings in heavenly places in Christ: According as He hath chosen us in Him before the foundation of the world, that we should be holy and without blame before Him in love: Having predestinated us unto the adoption of children by Jesus Christ to Himself, according to the good pleasure of His will, to the praise of the glory of His grace, wherein He hath made us accepted in the beloved. In whom we have redemption through His blood, the forgiveness of sins, according to the riches of His grace;

I John 5:11-13

And this is the record, that God hath given to us eternal life, and this life is in His Son, He that hath the Son hath life; and He that hath not the Son of God hast not life. These things have I written unto you that believe on the name of the Son of God; that ye may know that ye have eternal life, and that ye may believe on the name of the Son of God.

Colossians 1:12-13

Giving thanks unto the Father, which hath made us meet to be partakers of the inheritance of the saints in light: who hath delivered us from the power of darkness and translated us into the Kingdom of His dear Son.

God qualifies man as a partaker of kingdom benefits. He literally establishes man into the kingdom of God and establishes His kingdom in man. There is no sickness in the kingdom of God; no poverty; no guilt; no shame, no chaos in the kingdom of God. God desires to carry out rulership on this earth through man. Man must realize who he is, and what rightfully belongs to him as a citizen of heaven, and as a child of God, as he studies God's Word. God's rulership on planet earth must come through regenerated or born again man. This is why God said in **Luke 17:21,** *"Neither shall they say, lo here! for, behold the kingdom of God is within you."*

I John 3:1-3

Behold, what manner of love the Father hath bestowed upon us, that we should be called the sons of God: therefore the world knoweth us not, because it knew him not. Beloved, now are we the sons of God, and it doth not yet appear what we shall be: but we know that, when he shall appear, we shall be like him; for we shall see him as he is. And every man that hath this hope in him purifieth himself, even as he is pure.

God has a reason and purpose for all decisions He makes. He does not haphazardly do anything. When God created Adam and Eve, He made them rulers. After Adam and Eve sinned, satan took the rulership of earth. There was only one way God could legally rule in planet earth. He made a decision to live within redeemed man in the person of the Holy Spirit. Today, God rules in the earth realm through redeemed man. This is why we, as believers, must be governed by the Word of God. Our lives no longer belong to us, after Jesus is made Lord of our lives. We forfeit the right to do as we please. We purpose to do only as He wills. We give up our rights in exchange for His predesigned plan and purpose for our lives. We yield to Him and accept a new life in Him.

Galatians 2:20

I am crucified with Christ: nevertheless I live; yet not I, but Christ liveth in me: and the life which I now live in the flesh I live by the faith of the Son of God, who loved me, and gave Himself for me.

Colossians 3:1-3

If ye then be risen with Christ, seek those things which are above, where Christ sitteth on the right hand of God. Set your affection on things above, not on things on the earth. For ye are dead, and your life is hid with Christ in God.

Ephesians 1:3-6

Blessed be the God and Father of our Lord Jesus Christ, who hath blessed us with all spiritual blessings in heavenly places in Christ: according as He hath chosen us in Him before the foundation of the world, that we should be holy and without blame before Him in love: having predestinated us unto the adoption of children by Jesus Christ to Himself, according to the good pleasure of His will, to the praise of the glory of His grace, wherein He hath made us accepted in the Beloved.

God knows every person who will ever walk planet earth. Before He fashioned the world, He chose us and preordained that we should be born again of His Spirit. God made us to represent Him in the earth to the praise of His glory. Because of the unmerited favor He extended to all mankind, we are free to worship Him and serve Him. He accepted us in Himself. This is why we must accept ourselves and realize that our significance, worth and purpose is founded in Him. We come to realize daily who we really are in His Presence, and who He really is as we fellowship and commune with Him. We think His thoughts as we examine what is in the mind of God. We know what is in the mind of God as we study the Word of God. The Bible reveals the mind of God to re-created man. No book could contain all that is in the mind of God, but God has given us that measure of His Word required for us to communicate with Him effectively, and live out His ordinances here on planet earth. He has revealed the truth of His Word to give stability, direction, and strength to our lives.

II Corinthians 3:18

But we all, with open face beholding as in a glass the glory of the Lord, are changed into the same image from glory to glory, even as by the Spirit of the Lord.

II Corinthians 5:14-21

For the love of Christ constraineth us; because we thus judge, that if one died for all, then were all dead: and that he died for all, that they which live should not henceforth live unto themselves, but unto him which died for them, and rose again. Wherefore henceforth know we no man after the flesh: yea, though we have known Christ after the flesh, yet now henceforth know we him no more. Therefore if any man be in Christ, he is a new creature: old things are passed away; behold, all things are become new. And all things are of God who hath reconciled us to himself by Jesus Christ, and hath given to us the ministry of reconciliation; to wit, that God was in Christ, reconciling the world unto himself, not imputing their trespasses unto them; and hath committed unto us the word of reconciliation. Now then we are ambassadors for Christ, as though God did beseech you by us: we pray you in Christ's stead, be ye reconciled to God. For he hath made him to be sin for us, who knew no sin; that we might be made the righteousness of God in him.

Romans 12:1-3

I beseech you therefore, brethren, by the mercies of God, that ye present your bodies a living sacrifice, holy, acceptable unto God, which is your reasonable service. And be not conformed to this world: but be ye transformed by the renewing of your mind, that ye may prove what is that good, and acceptable, and perfect, will of God. For I say, through the grace given unto me, to every man that is among you, not to think of himself more highly than he ought to think; but to think soberly, according as God hath dealt to every man the measure of faith.

Jesus paid the ultimate price to re-establish man's relationship with God and rulership in the earth. God set his heart upon mankind in such a measure that He placed him in a class with himself to oversee the works of His hands. Redeemed man is in the same class with God. He is filled with the Spirit of God and authorized to set things in order in this earth. God wants to display the magnificence of His power through redeemed man. He establishes His kingdom in this earth. God is limited by what He can do in this earth only if <u>we</u> limit Him. He must have an available vessel; one that is yielded to Him in order to reveal an unquestionable manifestation of His power. This is why He has given us His authority, His inherent ability, and His Word.

Today we are the sons and daughters of God because of the blood of Jesus Christ. How can we deny such a great gift? Our Father has given us joint authority with Jesus, joint-heirship with Jesus, joint position with Jesus. Our position today is not a poverty stricken, deprived status in life, but rather a position of joint rulership with the Lord Jesus Christ.

Revelation 1:6
And hath made us kings and priests unto God and his Father; to Him be glory and dominion for ever and ever. Amen.

Romans 8:15
For ye have not received the spirit of bondage again to fear; but ye have received the Spirit of adoption, whereby we cry, Abba, Father.

We can only be sustained in this life by the Word of God and the power of the Holy Spirit. This is why I have verified many statements, not with my opinion, but the living Word of God. It is the Word of God that is alive, operative, active and full of power, not my experience or opinion. **John 6:63** says, *"It is the Spirit that quickeneth; the flesh profiteth nothing: the words that I speak unto you, they are spirit, and they are life."*

The following scriptures verify our position in God. If we believe the Bible, we must not only read and speak it, but live it as well. The acquisition of knowledge without application is futile. Wisdom is the application of knowledge.

Knowledge has one source, God. We can get information from many sources. We can only get the truth (knowledge) from God, who is all knowledge. Knowledge gained is good, but knowledge in and of itself does not transform. This is why so many believers are frustrated and defeated in life. They spend endless hours acquiring a vast resource of information, yet are void of true spiritual knowledge. Spiritual knowledge comes from God. This knowledge of spiritual things is of no benefit unless it is implemented. Therefore, all believers need a knowledge of spiritual things, which is truth. Full knowledge applied, is wisdom in its fullest expression. It is not the one who acquires the Word that reaps the benefits, but rather the doer of the Word he has acquired, who reaps the benefits.

James 1:22-25

But be ye doers of the word, and not hearers only, deceiving your own selves. For if any be a hearer of the word, and not a doer, he is like unto a man beholding his natural face in a glass: for he beholdeth himself, and goeth his way, and straightway forgetteth what manner of man he was. But whoso looketh into the perfect law of liberty, and continueth therein, he being not a forgetful hearer, but a doer of the work, this man shall be blessed in his deed.

Ephesians 2:10

And you hath he quickened, who were dead in trepasses and sins; wherein time past ye walked according to the course of this world, according to the prince of the power of the air, the spirit that now worketh in the children of disobedience: among whom also we all had our conversation in times past in the lust of our flesh, fulfilling the desires of the flesh and of the mind; and were by nature the children of wrath even as others. But God, who is rich in mercy, for His great love wherewith He loved us, even when we were dead in sins, hath quickened us together with Christ, (by grace ye are saved;) and hath raised us up together, and made us sit together in heavenly places in Christ Jesus that in the ages to come He might shew the exceeding riches of His grace in His kindness toward us through Christ Jesus. For by grace are ye saved through faith; and that not of yourselves: it is the gift of God: not of works, lest any should boast for we are his workmanship, created in Christ Jesus unto good works, which God hath before ordained that we should walk in them.

I Peter 2:9-10

But ye are a chosen generation, a royal priesthood, an holy nation, a peculiar people; that ye should shew forth the praises of him who hath called you out of darkness into his marvelous light: which in time past were not a people, but are now the people of God: which had not obtained mercy, but now have obtained mercy.

Our position of rulership has been re-established and the Word of God reveals exactly who we are. Our lives today must be founded on the truth of God's Word. It is the truth that we know that makes us free and he whom the Son makes free, is free indeed. To know truth simply means that one has entered into absolute harmonic agreement with God. The word "know" implies that one has established a relationship with. You and I must enter into active participation with God's Word. We must live the Word. God's Word must be visible for others to see and desire God. Sight breeds desire.

John 8:32 – 36

And ye shall know the truth, and the truth shall make you free. They answered him, We be Abraham's seed, and were never in bondage to any man: how sayest thou, Ye shall be made free? Jesus answered them, Verily, verily, I say unto you, Whosoever committeth sin is the servant of sin. And the servant abideth not in the house for ever: but the Son abideth ever. If the Son therefore shall make you free, ye shall be free indeed.

II Corinthians 3:1-5

Do we begin again to commend ourselves? or need we, as some others, epistles of commendation to you, or letters of commendation from you? Ye are our epistle written in our hearts, known and read of all men: Forasmuch as ye are manifestly declared to be the epistle of Christ ministered by us, written not with ink, but with the Spirit of the living God; not in tables of stone, but in fleshy tables of the heart. And such trust have we through Christ to God-ward: Not that we are sufficient of ourselves to think any thing as of ourselves; but our sufficiency is of God;

In His Presence

*I*n the spiritual sense, believers are always in the presence of God. If we stay in constant fellowship with the Lord, we abide in His presence. Often, our fellowship is interrupted by sin. Sin will always separate man from the Presence of God. If a man will keep himself from sin, he will enjoy constant communion with the Lord. God has made the body of the believer His dwelling place and has placed the anointing (His Spirit) within the believer. Daily, as we fellowship with the Lord, our relationship and fellowship with Him intensifies.

I Corinthians 3:16
Know ye not that ye are the temple of God, and that the Spirit of God dwelleth in you?

I John 2:20-27
But ye have an unction from the Holy One, and ye know all things. I have not written unto you because ye know not the truth, but because ye know it, and that no lie is of the truth. Who is a liar but he that denieth that Jesus is the Christ? He is antichrist, that denieth the Father and the Son. Whosoever denieth the Son, the same hath not the Father: (but) he that acknowledgeth the Son hath the Father also. Let that therefore abide in you, which ye have heard from the beginning. If

*that which ye have heard from the beginning
shall remain in you, ye also shall continue
in the Son, and in the Father. And this is
the promise that He hath promised us, even
eternal life. These things have I written unto
you concerning them that seduce you. But
the anointing which ye have received of Him
abideth in you, and ye need not that any man
teach you: but as the same anointing teacheth
you of all things and is truth, and is no lie
even as it hath taught you, ye shall abide in
Him.*

The above scriptures simply reveal the presence of the
Holy Spirit, who is the Spirit of God, within the believer.
The Bible says we have an unction from the Holy One. The
word unction comes from the Greek word "chrisma" which
means separated to God; it is the power which enables a
Christian to live holy, possessing a knowledge of truth. This
unction or power of God refers to the anointing of the Holy
Spirit placed within the believer. The Holy Spirit empowers
us to resist the pull, the power and the persuasion of sin.
The anointing is the power of God and again represents the
presence of the Holy Spirit, who is the Teacher. He comes to
reveal truth to the believer and enable the believer to discern
truth from error. The Bible is not saying we cannot be taught
by other members of the Body of Christ. It simply states that
the Holy Spirit is the Spirit of Truth. He is the revealer of
truth. Therefore, believers should not allow themselves to
follow after false doctrine, or seducers (those who come to
deceive with religious philosophies of men). God empowers
His children to rightly divide the Word of truth. Just because
a person is religious, does not mean they are saved, or born
again.

John 14:16-17

And I will pray the Father and He shall give you another Comforter, that he may abide with you for ever; even the Spirit of truth; whom the world cannot receive, because it seeth him not, neither knoweth him: but ye know him; for he dwelleth with you, and shall be in you.

John 14:26

But the Comforter, which is the Holy Ghost, whom the Father will send in my name, he shall teach you all things, and bring all things to your remembrance, whatsoever I have said unto you.

I John 4:1-4

Beloved, believe not every spirit, but try the spirits whether they are of God: because many false prophets are gone out into the world. Hereby know ye the Spirit of God: every spirit that confesseth that Jesus Christ is come in the flesh is of God: and every spirit that confesseth not that Jesus Christ is come in the flesh is not of God: and this is that spirit of antichrist, whereof ye have heard that it should come; and even now already is it in the world. Ye are of God, little children, and have overcome them: because greater is He that is in you, than he that is in the world.

In the old dispensation, (before the death, burial, resurrection, and ascension of Christ) men did not have the Holy Spirit living within them as we have Him within us today. However, there are some common elements experienced by every man who has an encounter with God. These elements are conviction, cleansing, conversion, and commission. In the case of Isaiah, the Bible reveals these elements. Isaiah finds himself in the presence of an awesome God. His own sinfulness is exposed, thus, he experiences conviction, which is the act of convincing one of error and compels the individual to acknowledge the truth about himself. The greatness of God, the glory of God, the power of God and the Word of God always brings conviction to the person who comes face to face with God. The Bible speaks of God's train, which is the glory of God, filling the temple. Isaiah acknowledges he is wretched and not only needs God, but purifying as well. He says, "Woe is me for I am undone, because I am a man of unclean lips and I dwell in the midst of a people of unclean lips." His human frailties are exposed before his eyes. In the presence of God he experiences cleansing and conversion. Then he makes a decision to accept God as the true source of life and mercy. Isaiah accepts the commission to go and obey God in all things.

Isaiah 6:1-8

In the year that king Uzziah died I saw also the Lord sitting upon a throne, high and lifted up, and his train filled the temple. Above it stood the seraphims: each one had six wings; with twain he covered his face, and with twain he covered his feet and with twain he did fly. And one cried unto another, and said, holy, holy, holy, is the Lord of hosts: the whole earth is full of His glory. And the posts of the door moved at the voice of him that cried, and the house was filled with smoke. Then said I, woe is me? for I am undone; because I am a man of unclean lips, and I dwell in the midst of a people of unclean lips: for mine eyes have seen the King, the Lord of hosts. Then flew one of the seraphims unto me, having a live coal in his hand, which he had taken with the tongs from off the altar: and he laid it upon my mouth, and said, Lo, this hath touched thy lips; and thine iniquity is taken away, and thy sin purged. Also I heard the voice of the Lord, saying, whom shall I send, and who will go for us? then said I, here am I; send me.

Man always experiences true conviction when he stands face to face with God. Isaiah realized that He could do all God assigned him to do after he had been touched by the purifying fire of God. In God's presence we see ourselves in light of truth. We are exposed before Almighty God. We are also exposed before our own eyes. It is in the face of holiness that one cries as David, *create in me a clean heart, O God, and renew the right spirit within me* (**Psalm 51:10**).

Job 42:1-6

Then Job answered the Lord, and said, I know that thou canst do everything, and that no thought can be withholden from thee. Who is he that hideth counsel without knowledge? Therefore have I uttered that I understood not; things too wonderful for me, which I knew not. Hear, I beseech thee, and I will speak: I will demand of thee, and declare thou unto me. I have heard of thee by the hearing of the ear: but now mine eye seeth thee. Wherefore I abhor myself, and repent in dust and ashes.

Acts 9:3-6

*And as he journeyed, he came near
Damascus: and suddenly there shined round
about him a light from heaven: And he fell to
the earth, and heard a voice saying unto him,
Saul, Saul, why persecutest thou me? And
he said, who art thou, Lord? And the Lord
said, I am Jesus whom thou persecutest: it is
hard for thee to kick against the pricks. And
he trembling and astonished said, Lord, what
wilt thou have me to do? And the Lord said
unto him, arise, and go into the city, and it
shall be told thee what thou must do.*

Being in the presence of God causes man to acknowledge
total and absolute dependence upon God. Only God can
open the eyes of those who are spiritually blind, convict
a man of sin, cleanse a man of sin, then bring conversion
and preparation for commission. It is awesome to see what
actually happens when we enter the presence of God.
Proverbs 20:27 says, *"the spirit of man is the candle of
the Lord, searching all the inward parts of the belly."* The
belly refers to man's innermost being or innermost counsel.
God uses His Word as a light to search out the inward part
of man and expose what is within. It is by searching man
that God brings to light what is in man. God knows what
is in every creature, but He exposes the inside in order that
every man and every woman might see himself or herself
in light of truth before a holy and just God. Notice the cry
of Isaiah, Job and Saul (later named Paul). Each recognizes
flaws in his own character. Each feels compelled to
obedience after being in the Lord's presence. Each man
examines himself before the greatness of God. Let's look
at another individual.

Exodus 33:11-23

And the Lord spake unto Moses face to face, as a man speaketh unto his friend. And he turned again into the camp: but his servant Joshua, the son of Nun, a young man, departed not out of the tabernacle. And Moses said unto the Lord, See, thou sayest unto me, bring up this people: and thou hast not let me know whom thou wilt send with me. Yet thou hast said, I know thee by name, and thou hast also found grace in my sight. Now therefore, I pray thee, if I have found grace in thy sight, shew me now thy way, that I may know thee, that I may find grace in thy sight: and consider that this nation is thy people. And He said, <u>My presence</u> shall go with thee, and I will give thee rest. And he said unto him, if <u>thy presence</u> go not with me, carry us not up hence. For wherein shall it be known here that I and thy people have found grace in thy sight? Is it not in that thou goest with us? So shall we be separated, I and thy people, from all the people that are upon the face of the earth. And the Lord said unto Moses, I will do this thing also that thou hast spoken: for thou hast found grace in my sight, and I know thee by name. And he said, I beseech thee, shew me thy glory. And he said, I will make all my goodness pass before thee, and I will proclaim the name of the Lord before thee; and will be gracious to who I will be gracious and, will shew mercy on whom I will shew mercy. And he said, thou canst not see my face: for there shall no man see me, and live.

And the Lord said, Behold, there is a place by me, then thou shalt stand upon a rock: and it shall come to pass, while my glory passeth by, that I will put thee in a clift of the rock, and will cover thee with my hand while I pass by: and I will take away mine hand, and thou shalt see my back parts; but my face shall not be seen.

God says **His presence** will go with Moses and He promises to give Moses rest. What is this rest? Rest is a state of calm assurance that God will perform that which He has vowed. It is simply child-like trust in a faithful God. God gives us rest (peace) and ease of spirit. Moses experiences this ease of spirit because he is confidently assured that God is on His side and will fully carry out the words He has spoken to Moses. Moses had no fear. Fear has torment and is paralyzing. It takes false evidence and causes it to appear real. God assured Moses he could trust Him. Whenever we fully rely on God, we experience perfect rest, perfect peace, no matter what is going on around us.

Moses speaks to God face to face, which tells us he was accustomed to communicating with God, because he knew God intimately. Moses spent much time with God. He experienced the miraculous power of God and had liberty in asking God to specifically do certain things for him. God committed Himself to His people and found pleasure in revealing Himself to them. When God was about to destroy Sodom and Gomorrah because of their grave wickedness, He remembered Abraham and said, *"Shall I hide from Abraham that thing which I do; seeing that Abraham shall surely become a great and mighty nation; and all the nations of the earth shall be blessed in him? For I know him, that he will command his children and his household after him, and they shall keep the way of the Lord, to do justice and judgment; that the Lord may bring upon Abraham that which he hath spoken of him* **(Genesis 18:17-19).**

Abraham developed such a relationship with God until, before God would make a major move of judgment against the wicked, He was compelled to tell Abraham about it first. God expressed the fact that He knew Abraham. He was intimately acquainted with Abraham and knew that Abraham would not only live upright before Him; but he would teach his children to live upright before God as well.

God is committed to His people. God wants to reveal to us those things that affect our lives. We must draw close to God so that we are always in a position to hear His voice. Look at what the Bible says in **Amos 3:7**, *"Surely the Lord God will do nothing, but he revealeth his secret unto his servants the prophets."* If you will make a decision to seek God with all your heart and allow your relationship with Him to be developed by constant communion with Him and study of His Word, you can depend on Him to reveal supernaturally astounding things to you; not just things about your life, but things that will happen in days to come.

The Word spoken in **Amos 3:7** was not just to those who walk in the office gift of the prophet, but to all those who are committed to God with their whole heart. Moses had this same assurance that God would prove himself faithful. You and I mean as much to God as Moses and Abraham. We too can experience this awesome privilege when our relationship with God is valued above all else. This is confirmed in *John 15:7* where Jesus says, *"If ye abide in me, and my words abide in you, ye shall ask what ye will, and it shall be done unto you."* He speaks of constant fellowship. A person whose life is governed by the Word of God, can ask God for things validated by the Word and have the assurance of receiving those things for which he asked. Why? Because we serve a God who gets glory when we receive answers to our prayers. God is able to reveal Himself as our God in answering our prayers.

God told Moses that he found grace in the sight of God. Moses asked God to reveal His ways to him. It is the will of God that we know His ways and His plan for our lives. He is Creator of all and surely He knows what He has called us to do. A powerful principle to draw from the request of Moses is, whenever you need an answer concerning the call of God on your life, ask the One who called you. Moses did not go to Jethro, his father-in-law or Joshua, his minister. He did not go to Aaron, his brother. Moses went straight to God when he needed instruction concerning what God had called him to do. You too, have been extended this awesome privilege. What God has called you to do, He will reveal to you. Remember, if it affects your life, God will not work independent of you and He is obligated by His Word to make His plan for your life crystal clear. We can never allow another person's decision or opinion to determine our destiny. We must persevere in all things and seek God for ourselves. God will confirm to others what He has already spoken to us.

When we seek God, we will always receive instruction, correction, revelation, comfort, refreshing, anointing, and deliverance. Revelation comes from a Greek word, "apokalipsis" which means to uncover, unveil or reveal. Obviously, God does not want us ignorant or unlearned in spiritual things. If He did, why does He give illumination to our minds and direction to our spirits? Why does He commit to reveal secrets and give us revelation? Why did He leave us **Genesis** to **Revelation** to read and adhere to? Look at the following scripture:

I Corinthians 2:9-12
But as it is written, eye hath not seen, nor ear heard, neither have entered into the heart of man, the things which God hath prepared for them that love him. But God hath revealed them unto us by His Spirit: for the Spirit searcheth all things, yea, the deep things of God. For what man knoweth the things of a man, save the spirit of man which is in him? Even so the things of God knoweth no man, but the Spirit of God. Now we have received not the spirit of the world, but the Spirit of God: that we might know the things that are freely given to us of God.

I believe a clear understanding of what God has created each person to accomplish, for the kingdom, is required before we can successfully complete any task delegated us by the Father. God shows us clearly and distinctly that He reveals all that He has purposed for our lives by His Spirit. Therefore, it is wise to conclude that God is not mysterious nor does He want to keep us ignorant of what He has prepared for His own. He may not reveal all things when we desire, but I believe in a step by step process, He unfolds His plan, in His own time.

Chapter Five

Jeremiah 29:11

For I know the thoughts that I think toward you, saith the Lord, thoughts of peace, and not of evil, to give you an expected end.

Those of you reading this book should always seek the face of God for fresh insight to direct your life. God's people cannot be spiritually nourished on just a pretty little sermon you heard someone preach. Sure, we draw wisdom from others in ministry and share what we learn from others, but it should not be a practice of always depending on something we heard from someone else. We need to research the Word and study it for ourselves. The Holy Spirit is the Teacher for every member of the Body of Christ.

There are no new revelations or deep revelations. God's Word is revelation. It is fresh and it is alive. As we develop spiritually, and mature in the things of God, we develop clearer insight into the things God has already revealed in His Word. The Holy Spirit gives us in-depth insight in the ways and the plans of God. He will do this with anyone who is committed to seriously study the Word of God and be a doer of the Word. God is not dropping out new revelations. He floods the eyes of our spiritual understanding with light, illumination or spiritual understanding as we labor in **His Presence** and in His Word. As we mature, walking in what God has already made known, He opens up more of His Word to us. I have heard many say, "God's Word gives birth to new facets of revelation." I believe what actually happens is that as God's people begin to develop spiritually, their perception or spiritual awareness of kingdom realities is enlightened in a greater measure than ever before. The more we mature and develop in the things of God, the more the Holy Spirit is able to reveal. He is able to reveal, uncover, or unveil what God has for His people, in a dimension many have not yet experienced. In essence, we come into the full knowledge of the Son of God, unto a perfect (spiritually mature) man, unto the measure of the stature of the fullness of Christ:...(**Ephesians 4:13**) Full knowledge comes from the Greek word "**epignosis**." God wants all of His children to walk in the fullness of knowledge. He wants us to have comprehensive insight into His ways and purposes.

God called us to minister (which actually means to serve) His people fresh bread. His people need fresh Word. This fresh Word for today can only come from the heart of God, and we can only know what is in the heart of God as we labor in **His Presence,** and fellowship with Him through study of the scriptures. Jesus said, *"I am the Bread of Life,"* **(John 6:35).** We must become acquainted with the Bread of life. Only He knows the needs of His people. Christians must always abide in the presence of God. We cannot serve God's people if we are not prepared. To direct God's people, we must stay before God and receive constant insight from God. Let me say again, you can only receive instruction from the heart of God, when you have been in **His Presence**.

Anybody can preach (proclaim) a message they heard someone else preach, but very few can literally minister (serve) to God's people from the heart of God. Why? Because only a select few will petition God concerning His heart-beat for His people. When Moses was commissioned by God to deliver the children of Israel out of bondage, he specifically asked God who he should say sent him. He wanted the answer directly from the mouth of God. What he had heard about God was not sufficient.

Exodus 3:13-14

And Moses said unto God, behold, when I come unto the children of Israel, and shall say unto them, the God of your fathers hath sent me unto you; and they shall say to me, what is his name? What shall I say unto them? And God said unto Moses, I AM THAT I AM: and He said, thus shalt thou say unto the children of Israel, I AM hath sent me unto you.

Moses asked God to reveal His ways so that he could know Him. The believer must always seek to know God's ways, because he wants to know God, not because he seeks to impress men. He must seek God's ways because, as Moses, he is helpless without divine direction. It is never enough to just possess head knowledge of supernatural things or know the mechanics of the supernatural. Knowing the mechanics does not bring power or success. Too many possess a head knowledge of the Bible and no relationship with God. Head knowledge will not help when the forces of evil rush in like a volcano that has just erupted. It is that personal one on one relationship with God that brings peace, even in the worst of situations. **Failure is inevitable without God**. God knows the hearts and minds of all men, even as He knew the heart of Moses and only the power of God, evident from being in His presence, can bring victory and give peace in chaotic situations.

After asking to know the ways of God, Moses asked to see God's glory. Moses had no fear **in the presence of God**. He was dependent upon God for direction and sought assurance. He was consumed with glorifying God and boldly told God that he did not want to lead God's people, if God was not present with him. Why? All of us are utterly helpless without God. **Failure is imminent without the presence of God**. Many enjoy major achievements and acquire great materialistic riches and they attempt to equate this to success. There is no success without God regardless of what a man has.

God agreed to only allow His glory to pass by Moses, and for Moses to see his back parts. The full glory of God and the face of God in its majestic splendor and holiness was too powerful, too great for Moses or any man to behold. In this we see the protective hand of God. Even today, God will only reveal a measure of His glory before His people. We could never truly endure the fullness of God's glory in this earth-suit, or earthen vessel of clay.

Exodus 34:29-33

And it came to pass, when Moses came down from Mount Sinai with the two tables of testimony in Moses hand, when he came down from the mount, that Moses wist not that the skin of his face shone while he talked with him. And when Aaron and all the children of Israel saw Moses, behold, the skin of his face shone; and they were afraid to come nigh him. And Moses called unto them; and Aaron and all the rulers of the congregation returned unto him: and Moses talked with them. And afterward all the children of Israel came nigh: and he gave them in commandment all that the Lord had spoken with him in Mount Sinai. And till Moses had done speaking with them, he put a veil on his face.

It is evident that Moses had been in the presence of God, for his countenance radiated the glory of God. In these in-times, if we seek the face of God as never before, and linger in **His Presence**, surely the aroma of the presence of God will linger on us, and the glory of God will be revealed before all men. The scripture says, *"It is Christ in us, the hope of glory"* *(Colossians 1:27).* We stand as God's representatives in this earth and if we dwell in the presence of God, all men will know we have been with God.

These are the days in which every child of God needs to dwell in the presence of God. No, this is not an impossibility. Man can live in the presence of God, all day long if he chooses. Look at what the Psalmist was inspired to write. He speaks of continually abiding in the presence of God.

Psalm 91:1-2

He that dwelleth in the secret place of the most High shall abide under the shadow of the Almighty. I will say of the Lord, He is my refuge and my fortress: My God, in Him will I trust.

We can experience the glory of God, and the protective care of the Almighty, as we purpose in our hearts to consistently dwell in the secret place of the Most High. Where is this place? It's simply **in His presence**. This is why there is no distance in prayer, for the presence of God is within us. The Presence of God is within the spirit of born-again believers. This is why the Bible speaks of the believer's body as the temple of God. God does not dwell in temples made of brick and mortar. We have this treasure in earthen vessels and He is only a prayer away, a whisper away. We can ever live in a state of prayer.

II Corinthians 4:7
*But we have this treasure in earthen vessels,
that the excellency of the power may be of
God, and not of us.*

God uniquely designed us to long for Him as Creator
and Father. He fashioned us to live **in His Presence,** and
living **in His Presence** simply means we are in constant
fellowship and communion with Him. The anointing, which
is the power of Almighty God, saturates us as we enter His
Presence. This is why the face of Moses was radiant with the
glory of God. No man can abide in the presence of God and
not be arrayed with the anointing of God.

When a man experiences the presence of God, others
will be affected by the aroma that comes from that one who
has labored before God. The Spirit of God revealed to me
that many believers have so many yokes in their own lives
because there is no anointing. There is no anointing because
they have not labored **in the presence of God**. They neglect
His presence and it is **in His presence** that we draw from
the anointing which destroys every yoke of bondage. A
life void of the anointing cannot experience liberty in God
(**II Corinthians 3:17**). The anointing brings deliverance,
it brings freedom. The anointing empowers for change, it
influences change. God has designed man to respond to the
anointing. The anointing produces something far greater
than the spectacular. It stirs the heart and reaches deep
within the spirit of man driving out every entangling yoke of
bondage. Even Moses recognized that it takes the anointing
to successfully fulfill God's call upon one's life.

Man may do a few good works without the fullness
of the anointing, but he will never experience maximum

potential. The anointing does so much more than just break yokes of bondage. The anointing penetrates, thrusts through, and transcends man's natural limitations. Many speak of the anointing breaking the yoke. God wants more than broken yokes. To break simply means to separate in parts or lessen the potential value or threat of. The essence of God's anointing is to destroy, literally annihilate every yoke. A yoke is characterized as a form of bondage, or enslavement. It keeps man from experiencing the fullness of God. It is initiated by satan and designed ultimately to destroy. God's power, the anointing, is available to destroy the yoke. Man will not experience total and absolute freedom apart from God's presence because the anointing is captured **in His presence**. No man has a monopoly on the anointing, the power of God. It cannot be bought and it cannot be sold. It is strictly given by God to those who commit their lives to Him and He bestows it in whatever magnitude or degree He chooses for His own glory.

God said many have yokes of bondage in their lives because there is no anointing. Fresh anointing comes from abiding in the presence of God, and it is the anointing that destroys the yoke.

Isaiah 10:27

And it shall come to pass in that day, that his burden shall be taken away from off thy shoulder, and his yoke from off thy neck, and the yoke shall be destroyed because of the anointing.

Let me just mention that fasting does not change God, it changes men. The potential strength of yokes can be weakened or lessened in intensity during fasting but fasting does not destroy the yokes of bondage. Fasting weakens yokes because the spirit man ascends and is more yielded to God, however, it is only the anointing that literally destroys the yoke.

Isaiah 58:6
Is not this the fast that I have chosen? To loose the bands of wickedness, to undo the heavy burdens, and to let the oppressed go free, and that ye break every yoke?

Psalm 55:22
Cast thy burden upon the Lord and he shall sustain thee: he shall never suffer the righteous to be moved.

God calls us to live **in His presence**. He does not want us to visit Him when difficulty arises. He wants us to literally abide daily **in His presence**. A person who tastes the presence of God in brief visits is dangerous. Why? Because they don't allow time for development. They sample the supernatural and take off without experiencing that fine balance that all believers must operate in. They are controlled more by the senses than they are led by the Holy Spirit. A person led by the Spirit will not neglect the power found in consistent communion and fellowship with God. Those who visit the presence of God are not spirit-led, but flesh ruled and the Bible says, *"there is no good thing in the flesh."* God says, in **I Corinthians 1:29** *"...no flesh should glory in His presence."* To become spirit-ruled is a decision, not a biblical occurrence. A person has to make a decision to live in the presence of God, and discipline himself to seek the face of God. This is how fellowship with God is intensified, and man is kept from the entrapment of satan.

I would like to share some profound truths God revealed to me during a time of prayer. As I prayed, I sensed such a tremendous burden. I began to examine myself before God and ask Him, what is this that I am experiencing. I was in church interceding just before the services began, with other members of the Body of Christ. His words to me were, *"My people cannot neglect My presence all week long and then expect to experience the anointing."* God said, *"My people neglect Me daily, then congregate on occasions and literally drain the man or woman of God because they want to experience the anointing, the supernatural. Yet, they don't want to position themselves in a place to hear from Me daily."* Tears began to swell in my eyes as I listened to what God was saying. Many want to see miracles, and many desire the blessings of God to overtake them. God says, *"My people will not experience victory, deliverances, or change apart from My presence."*

When I experienced a time of great emptiness in my own life, I began to seek the face of God. It was during this time that I asked the Lord what was this dis-satisfaction I was experiencing; and God said, *"What you are experiencing is spiritual drought."* A spiritual drought or spiritual famine comes as a result of failure to consistently abide in the presence of God. David so beautifully explains this experience.

Psalm 63:1-7

O God, thou art my God; early will I seek thee: my soul thirsteth for thee, my flesh longeth for thee in a dry and thirsty land, where no water is; to see thy power and thy glory, so as I have seen thee in the sanctuary. Because thy loving kindness is better than life, my lips shall praise thee. Thus will I bless thee while I live: I will lift up my hands in thy name. My soul shall be satisfied as with marrow and fatness; and my mouth shall praise thee with joyful lips: when I remember thee upon my bed, and meditate on thee in the night watches. Because thou hast been my help, therefore in the shadow of thy wings will I rejoice. My soul followeth hard after thee: thy right hand upholdeth me.

The first powerful sentence in the above scripture identifies David as having a personal relationship with the Lord. It is because of this relationship that David says, ***"early will I seek thee."*** Early simply means beforehand, first and foremost. It can also mean early in life or early in the morning. I believe David positioned himself in a place to seek God first and foremost as well as early in his life. David had experienced the power of God. He knew what it was to bask in the glory of God. The thirst David speaks of is a sensation of dryness associated with a desire or yearning for fulfillment. His thirst, as with many believers was a famishing, all consuming craving and passion of spirit for complete union with God. He speaks of a spiritual condition that cannot be understood with the natural mind. Dry and thirsty land, symbolizes a condition of spiritual drought. David is in the wilderness of Judah when he writes this Psalm. While in this wilderness geographically, he experiences a longing within for the presence of God. He longs for the glory of God, the power of God. He longs to experience the loving kindness of God, all that God has to offer. He realizes that fulfillment and satisfaction comes from God no matter what the challenge, and no matter what the geographic locality. It is only when we search for God with our whole heart that we find Him.

Often we have found ourselves trying to satisfy the deep void and emptiness we experience with so many things. Yet we still experience a sense of longing or lack of fulfillment. I often wonder why many of our services are not filled with people when it is time to pray. God said to me, *"Many lack the thirst and hunger for My presence and you cannot put the hunger in My people for My presence. Even as I have drawn you by My Spirit, they must be drawn by Me and not resist My call. They must become so thirsty that they choose to search for Me with their whole hearts and follow my leading."* From that day to this present moment I have watched and observed. Certainly, if God does not put the hunger in a person to seek and desire His face, they will wander aimlessly in life, void of true fulfillment and life as God has ordained. Once God gives the hunger it must be responded to.

Jeremiah 29:11-14

For I know the thoughts that I think toward you, saith the Lord, thoughts of peace, and not of evil, to give you an expected end. Then shall ye call upon me, and ye shall go and pray unto me, and I will hearken unto you. And ye shall seek me, and find me, when ye shall search for me with all your heart. And I will be found of you, saith the Lord: and I will turn away your captivity, and I will gather you from all the nations, and from all the places whither I have driven you, saith the Lord; and I will bring you again into the place whence I caused you to be carried away captive.

God assures us that if we will seek Him, we will find Him. Perhaps, you are wondering, how do I seek God? To seek God is not difficult. Just make it a priority in your life to spend time studying God's Word and talking to Him just as you talk with others. Don't put on any pretenses, for God knows the heart. You don't have to major in grammar or correct word usage. Talk to the Lord as you would a loved one. Be yourself and allow God to be God in your life. He is not hiding from you, nor is He spooky or mystical. The more you take time to talk to Him, you will find that He will help you. He will guide you. He will give you instruction. Before I really knew how to communicate with the Lord by His Word, I took a book entitled "Prayers That Avail Much," and read the prayers to God. I did this so frequently until the words literally became a part of me. I don't need that book to pray according to God's Word any longer, because now the Word rises up within me as I seek my Father's face.

What I have just mentioned is extremely important for new babes in the Lord, because God honors praying in the spirit (other tongues) and prayer founded upon His Word. God does not honor the prayer that is filled with doubt and unbelief. He cannot, because He is a God of faith. He cannot honor prayers built upon the philosophies of men. He honors the prayer that is established by His Word, for He is His Word, and He will always honor His Own Word. God does not honor the lustful expectations and opinions of men.

As we look further into **Jeremiah 29:11-14**, many of you reading this book need to know God has an expected end for you. He has established your end from the beginning. He has predestined you to succeed in this life. His plan for you is sure, but you will not experience victory, deliverance, or fulfillment until you turn your face towards God by getting into His presence. Even though God has an expected end for you, the fulfillment of what God has for you is for an appointed time and only you, can hinder what God wants to do. Not even the forces of darkness can stop you from doing what God has formed you to do. It is important that your heart is pure before God, and that you purpose in your heart to walk in obedience before God in every area of life.

Psalm 66:18-20

If I regard iniquity in my heart, the Lord will not hear me: But verily God hath heard me: He hath attended to the voice of my prayer. Blessed be God, which hath not turned away my prayer, nor his mercy from me.

Psalm 139:23-24

Search me, O God, and know my heart: try me, and know my thoughts: And see if there be any wicked way in me, and lead me in the way everlasting.

Habakkuk 2:1-3

I will stand upon my watch, and set me upon the tower, and will watch to see what he will say unto me, and what I shall answer when I am reproved. And the Lord answered me, and said, write the vision, and make it plain upon tables, that he may run that readeth it. For the vision is yet for an appointed time, but at the end it shall speak, and not lie: though it tarry, wait for it because it will surely come, it will not tarry.

Even as God spoke to me, I admonish every reader to be encouraged, and know that God's Spirit is present with you, to give you the strength you need to labor **in His presence**. Too many of us experience difficulty in taking time with God. *"Do not be weary in well doing for in due season you will reap if you faint not."* **(Galatians 6:9)** There are seasons of conflict; and seasons of intense battle. But, when the battle is over there is always a harvest to reap and spoils to recover. Remember, it's not what we encounter in life that affects our destiny, but rather how we respond to what we encounter. Therefore, be steadfast in the midst of the battle. Delight yourself in the Lord, recognize the little things that steal your time, and keep you from fellowshipping with the Lord through prayer, praise and study of the Word. Purpose in your heart to be diligent concerning the things of God. You can dare to be different. As you are obedient to God, be assured, *"no good thing will He withhold from them who walk uprightly."* **(Psalm 84:11-12)** God is an all-consuming fire, you don't have to experience spiritual famine, if you are willing to feast **in His presence**. Take the time to rehearse the goodness of God. This builds reinforcement within you. Discipline yourself to pray daily and be assured that God will reward your time with Him.

You can be assured that total fulfillment comes from God. However, it's not enough to know fulfillment comes from God; we must seek to be fulfilled in Him. One of the major elements that hinder many believers from experiencing the greatest degree of spiritual fulfillment, is the lust of the flesh. It is man's desire to please himself and his dependence upon the flesh that hinders the flow of the anointing. Sin will always separate man from the presence of God and keep man from enjoying the optimum, maximum fulfillment.

We begin experiencing genuine satisfaction in life when we enter the presence of the Lord. It is in God's presence that we experience true fulfillment, genuine enthusiasm and real fullness of joy. Enthusiasm comes from the Greek word "enthousiasmos" which means God within, full of God or inspired by God. There is only one way man can know God and that is to abide in the presence of God. We walk in all the fullness of God when we abide in Him and His words abide in us. God is within the born-again believer. Let's go through the scriptures and examine countless benefits to the man and woman, who will make a conscious effort to live **in the presence of God**.

II Corinthians 4:16-17

For which cause we faint not; but though our outward man perish, yet <u>the inward man is renewed day by day</u>. For our light affliction which is but for a moment, worketh for us a far more exceeding and eternal weight of glory.

The word **renewed,** above, means refreshed or charged up. Even though we encounter challenges in this life, the inward man, the spirit of man is refreshed day by day. How? As we abide **in the presence of God**. We draw fresh strength to handle anything we encounter in life.

Psalm 16:11

Thou wilt shew me the path of life: in thy presence is fullness of joy: at thy right hand there are pleasures for evermore.

If a man will find the path of life, he can only find it in the presence of God. Many wander aimlessly in life with no direction because they do not take the time to abide in the presence of God. We must never forget that the blessings and plan God has for the believer's life is not an automatic occurrence. Jesus said, *"I am the way, the truth and the life."* **(John 14:6)** He further stated, *"I am come that they might have life and have it more abundantly."* **(John 10:10)** In man's search for significance, acceptance, success and so much more, the Bible clearly reveals, that, all we will ever need for fulfillment in life, begins with He who has life within Himself. Joy and pleasures are found **In His presence,** and these denote endless and immeasurable satisfaction. These benefits are limitless to those who seek the face of God, and have confidence in God's Word. His Word reveals the path of life. We find direction for life, and how to enjoy kingdom benefits. As we look in the Word of God, for God is His Word, and He has given us His Word to bring order to our lives.

During a critical time in the history of his people, Nehemiah wrote the following words as he was inspired by the Spirit of God:

Nehemiah 8:10
"...the joy of the Lord is my strength."

He wanted God's people to know, that, even in times of great difficulty and frustration, that strength was possible if the joy of the Lord was present. This joy could only come as a result of experiencing the presence of God, and this was experienced by fellowship with a faithful God. Why does joy bring strength? Joy is the spiritual force and is not contingent upon outward circumstances or conditions. Joy comes as a result of understanding the faithfulness of God revealed on behalf of His people. Joy comes from the Greek word, "Chara," and means delight; the ability to rejoice; confidently assured of God's power working on one's behalf.

John 15:11

These things have I spoken unto you, that my joy might remain in you, and that your joy might be full.

John 16:20-24

Verily, verily, I say unto you, That ye shall weep and lament, but the world shall rejoice: and ye shall be sorrowful, but your sorrow shall be turned into joy. A woman when she is in travail hath sorrow, because her hour is come: but as soon as she is delivered of the child, she remembereth no more the anguish, for joy that a man is born into the world. And ye now therefore have sorrow: but I will see you again, and your heart shall rejoice, and your joy no man taketh from you. And in that day ye shall ask me nothing. Verily, verily, I say unto you, Whatsoever ye shall ask the Father in my name, he will give it you. Hitherto have ye asked nothing in my name: ask, and ye shall receive, that your joy may be full.

I John 5:13-15

These things have I written unto you that believe on the name of the Son of God; that ye may know that ye have eternal life, and that ye may believe on the name of the Son of God. And this is the confidence that we have in him, that, if we ask anything according to his will, he heareth us: and if we know that he hear us, whatsoever we ask, we know that we have the petitions that we desired of him.

If we truly commit our way to the Lord, repent of evil, and seek the Lord, we will experience true revival, true refreshing. God makes a clear distinction between those who belong to Him, and those who do not. He summons His people into His presence, and says if we humble ourselves, enter His presence with one purpose in mind, and that is to seek His face; if we turn from our wicked ways, then He vows that we will not only hear from heaven, but He will grant our petitions. He vows to heal our land. God simply says, He is willing to perfect all that concerns us (**Psalm 138:8).** He promises to forgive our sins and see us totally innocent and blameless in His sight. What an **AWESOME GOD!**

Acts 3:19

Repent ye therefore, and be converted, that your sins may be blotted out, when the times of refreshing shall come from the presence of the Lord.

II Chronicles 7:14

If my people, which are called by my name, shall humble themselves, and pray, and seek my face, and turn from their wicked ways; then will I hear from heaven, and will forgive their sin, and will heal their land. Now mine eyes shall be open, and mine ears attentive unto the prayer that is in this place.

Chapter Five

Matthew 11:28-30

*0 Come unto me, all ye that labor and are
heavy laden, and I will give you rest. Take
my yoke upon you, and learn of me; for I am
meek and lowly in heart: and ye shall find
rest unto your souls. For my yoke is easy and
my burden is light.*

God's presence brings rest to the weary. Many are weary
in life because, they are void of rest in God. An individual
can only rest in God when he has fellowship with God. As
a result of that fellowship, God is given an opportunity to
bathe the believer in His love, and reveal the way out of
difficult situations. He responds to our needs because He
loves us. God speaks to bring peace and assurance, that, He
will perform His Word.

II Chronicles 32:7-8

*Be strong and courageous, be not afraid nor
dismayed for the king of Assyria, nor for all
the multitude that is with him: for there be
more with us than with him: With him is an
arm of flesh; but with us is the Lord our God
to help us, and to fight our battles. And the
people rested themselves upon the words of
Hezekiah king of Judah.*

Isaiah 28:12

*To whom he said, this is the rest wherewith ye
may cause the weary to rest; and this is the
refreshing: yet they would not hear.*

Psalm 42:1-4

*As the hart panteth after the water brooks,
so panteth my soul after thee, O God. My*

soul thirsteth for God, for the living God: when shall I come and appear before God? My tears have been my meat day and night, while they continually say unto me, where is thy God? When I remember these things, I pour out my soul in me: for I had gone with the multitude, I went with them to the house of God, with the voice of joy and praise, with a multitude that kept holyday.

The hart is the male of the red deer. This animal feeds near water. Whenever chased by an enemy he submerges himself in the waters, so that his scent might be lost and the enemy cannot continue to track him by his scent. His scent is lost once he gets into the water. Often he stays submerged as long as his breath allows, then swims down stream in the middle, so as not to touch the branches of trees on either side. If he is ever caught in a chase away from water, he longs for the water because he understands he will be killed unless he can find the water. The water covers the scent of the deer.

David exposes a powerful truth in this passage concerning the believer. He reveals how the believer is protected from and delivered out of trouble as he is submerged **in the presence of God.** Fellowship and communion with God always keeps supernatural help available. The devil is a worthy opponent. If we are in a battle with satan and not protected by the power of God we cannot win. He is a formidable foe. It is only our union with Christ that keeps the devil from devouring the righteous. Even as the hart, we must pant for the water of life, the living presence of God. We must thirst for God continually. Remember, our God is only a prayer away and in Him we experience continuous safety and fulfillment. We will die spiritually without the **presence of God.**

Chapter Five

I Peter 5:8-10

Be sober, be vigilant; because your adversary the devil, as a roaring lion, walketh about, seeking whom he may devour: whom resist steadfast in the faith, knowing that the same afflictions are accomplished in your brethren that are in the world. But the God of all grace, who hath called us unto his eternal glory by Christ Jesus, after that ye have suffered (endured through the test) a while, make you perfect, stablish, strengthen, settle you.

Psalm 91:14-16

Because he hath set his love upon me, therefore will I deliver him: I will set him on high, because he hath known my name. He shall call upon me, and I will answer him: I will be with him in trouble; I will deliver him, and honour him. With long life will I satisfy him, and shew him my salvation (delivering power).

Isaiah 26:9

With my soul have I desired thee in the night; yea, with my spirit within me will I seek thee early (first and foremost); for when thy judgments are in the earth, the inhabitants of the world will learn righteousness.

The greatest illuminations, the most powerful sermons, the clearest directions I have received from God have always come when I positioned myself in the Father's presence. Likewise, the greatest illuminations, insight, and so much more, you will ever receive, will come from you being **in**

the presence of God. No enemy can touch us as long as we abide **in the presence of God,** ever conscious that He is our refuge and strength. He is a very present help in times of trouble.

You have full liberty to enter God's presence unashamed, guiltless and absolutely innocent. Some fear condemnation when they have not lived in total obedience to God. If you disobey God, don't run away from God. He is the only one who forgives, forgets, and washes away the stench of sin.

- Run into **His Presence**.
- There is deliverance **in His Presence**.
- There is healing **in His Presence**.
- There is love, joy, and peace **in His Presence**.
- Whatever you need today, you can find it **in His Presence.**
- There is forgiveness **in His Presence**.

Hebrews 4:14-16
Seeing then that we have a great high priest, that is passed into the heavens, Jesus the Son of God, let us hold fast our profession. For we have not an high priest which cannot be touched with the feeling of our infirmities; but was in all points tempted like as we are, yet without sin. Let us therefore come boldly unto the throne of grace, that we may obtain mercy and find grace to help in time of need.

Hebrews 10:19-23
Having therefore, brethren, boldness to enter into the holiest by the blood of Jesus, by a new and living way, which he hath

*consecrated for us, through the veil, that is to
say his flesh; and having an high priest over
the house of God; let us draw near with a true
heart in full assurance of faith, having our
hearts sprinkled from an evil conscience, and
our bodies washed with pure water. Let us
hold fast the profession of our faith without
wavering; (for he is faithful that promised;)*

Chapter Six

Waiting on God
(Yieldedness)

Isaiah 40:28-31

Hast thou not known? hast thou not heard, that the everlasting God, the Lord, the Creator of the ends of the earth, fainteth not, neither is weary? There is no searching of his understanding. He giveth power to the faint; and to them that have no might he increaseth strength. Even the youths shall faint and be weary, and the young men shall utterly fall? But they that wait upon the Lord shall renew their strength; they shall mount up with wings as eagles; they shall run, and not be weary; and they shall walk, and not faint.

The word "wait" in the above verses comes from a Hebrew word "qavah" which means to expect or look for patiently. When we think of waiting on God, the Bible is not referring to a state of being without motion. The Bible speaks of man's watchful expectation of God performing His Word. When you and I wait upon God, we are living in daily expectation of God fulfilling what He has vowed. Man's heart is lifted up towards God in confidence, that, He will not fail His children. As Abraham, we stagger not at the promises of God through unbelief, but we are strong in faith and fully persuaded that what God has vowed, He is not only able to perform, but will perform in our lives (**Romans 4:20-21**). We must recognize God's position as God of our lives. He recognizes our position as children who are absolutely dependent on Him. Therefore, we enter His presence with praise and worship. This is our time together. We will not deny Him the praise, adoration, and love He deserves. He will not deny us all we need for Godly living on planet earth. We must listen attentively to hear His voice. There, **in His presence**, we find renewed vision, strength, refreshing, peace, the zeal we need to persevere, insight, and instruction.

Psalm 62:5-6

My soul, wait thou only upon God; for my expectation is from Him. He only is my rock and my salvation: He is my defense; I shall not be moved.

As we wait on God, we are experiencing something awesome, "yieldedness." Yieldedness is a total position of surrender before God. In its simplest form, it is symbolic to hands thrown up in the air, and a bowing of the knees. We visualize this position as we think of a person surrendering, but the surrender I speak of must be of the heart. To wait on God will do us no good, unless, we have purposed in our hearts to yield to that which He speaks. When a man yields to God, he says, "God I want what you want more than anything else, no matter what the price. I will do the will of God, not just that which is comfortable. I will not be a convenience minded believer, serving God when it is convenient, or as long as it does not conflict with my schedule."

Psalm 46:10

*Be still, and know that I am God: I will be
exalted among the heathen, I will be exalted
in the earth.*

There are times in every believer's life when stillness
before God is required. All too often we run into the presence
of God, do all the talking (usually begging) and then run
right out. We have failed to thank God for His goodness. We
fail to worship and praise Him just because He is God. We
fail to draw wisdom, revelation and instruction from Him.
We neither allow Him the courtesy of expressing what is in
His heart, nor what is on His mind. Did you know that God
has a heart? There are things He would love to say, if given
a moment to do so. Can you see how we have taken His love
and kindness for granted? All that He has done, is doing and
will do in days to come is not because we are so good. It
is because He is so good. He is understanding and patient
towards us. How can we deny and neglect so great a love as
this? God has called us to delight in Him and rejoice in His
goodness.

Psalm 37:3-7

*Trust in the Lord, and do good; so shalt thou
dwell in the land, and verily thou shalt be fed.
Delight thyself also in the Lord; and he shall
give thee the desires of thine heart. Commit
thy way unto the Lord; trust also in him; and
he shall bring it to pass. And he shall bring
forth thy righteousness as the light, and thy
judgment as the noonday. Rest in the Lord,
and wait patiently for him:...*

We are spirits, created not for this world, but for eternity;
and, for God. We cannot put our trust in traditions of men,

doctrines of devils, people, schemes, and plans. We must trust only in God. The most treasured of habits and hobbies can become a snare if we allow them to divert our loyalty and true commitment from God.

We must examine ourselves and not focus on others. This is the day of reckoning. Every believer must examine himself in light of the Word of God and ask, "Am I truly fellowshipping with the Lord just because He's God? Is my relationship with Him based on the benefits, or is my relationship based upon mutual love? You see, the benefits just come with the package. God wants us to truly worship Him for the great love where with He has loved us. We, who are the righteous, must give God thanks.

Psalm 140:13
Surely the righteous shall give thanks unto thy name: the upright shall dwell in thy presence.

God has a purpose for every person's life. However, even though God has a purpose for every life, the fulfillment of that purpose is not automatic. The key to every person fulfilling God's plan for his or her life must be found by abiding **in the presence of God**. There is more to laboring **in the presence of God** than many are aware of. Abiding **in the presence of God** is comprised of seeking the face of God, waiting before God and yielding to God in obedience. Often we seek God for answers, but we don't want to wait on God, nor do we want to yield to God when instruction and insight comes.

Yieldedness before God is the ability to give up one's own way for what God wants. It is ultimate obedience to God regardless of circumstances, the critics, or

92

adversities encountered. In order to yield to God, we must be extremely sensitive to the leading of the Spirit of God and totally dependent on God for guidance. God wants to speak to us particularly. Yieldedness causes us to say as Jesus said, *"I came not to do my own will but the will of My Father, who sent Me."* What God has called us to do must be more important than anything else we could want in life.

Philippians 3:7-10

But what things were gain to me, those I counted loss for Christ. Yea doubtless, and I count all things but loss for the excellency of the knowledge of Christ Jesus my Lord? For whom I have suffered the loss of all things, and do count them but dung, that I may win Christ, and be found in him, not having mine own righteousness, which is of the law, but that which is through the faith of Christ, the righteousness which is of God by faith: that I may know him, and the power of his resurrection, and the fellowship of his sufferings, being made conformable unto his death...

John 4:34

Jesus saith unto them my meat is to do the will of him that sent me and finish His work.

Proverbs 3:5-6

Trust in the Lord with all thine heart; and lean not unto thine own understanding. In all thy ways acknowledge him, and he shall direct thy paths.

It takes discipline to walk with God. Man's life is void and involved in an endless search until it is filled with God and His purpose for that life. Many experience a yearning for fulfillment which can only come through communion with God. God desires to teach us how to experience something more valuable than material wealth. He wants us to experience the wealth of His love. He wants spiritual things to take precedent over everything else in life. He does not want us to become totally engrossed in the acquisition of materialistic wealth and fail to acquire insight into the realm of the spirit. There is nothing wrong with wealth. God simply wants our confidence to be in Him, not our possessions. As the Spirit of God revealed the universal condition of many in the Body of Christ, God spoke these words in **Revelation 3:18,** *"I counsel thee to buy of me gold tried in the fire, that thou mayest be rich; and white raiment, that thou mayest be clothed, and that the shame of thy nakedness do not appear; and anoint thine eyes with eyesalve, that thou mayest see."*

Matthew 6:19-21

Lay not up for yourselves treasures upon earth, where moth and rust doth corrupt, and where thieves break through and steal: but lay up for yourselves treasures in heaven, where neither moth nor rust doth corrupt, and where thieves do not break through nor steal: for where your treasure is there will your heart be also.

Mark 8:34-37

And when he had called the people unto him with his disciples also, he said unto them, whosoever will come after me, let him deny himself, and take up his cross, and follow me.

*For whosoever will save his life shall lose it;
but whosoever shall lose his life for my sake
and the gospel's, the same shall save it. For
what shall it profit a man, if he shall gain the
whole world, and lose his own soul? or what
shall a man give in exchange for His soul.*

Have you ever wondered what God is actually saying in
the above scriptures? He simply says, "Love me like I love
you." Remember God's total reason for creating man. He
wanted fellowship. He wanted someone exactly like Himself
to love Him by choice, with the same caliber of love by
which He loves. God designed man with the capacity to love
just like God. He wants us to commit to Him, like He has
committed Himself to us. Jesus gave up His life in order that
we might have life; and not just life, but life in the highest
form, to be enjoyed here now and eternally with Him in
heaven. If we put Him first and love Him because of who He
is, He will freely give us all things.

Romans 8:32
*He that spared not his own Son, but delivered
him up for us all, how shall he not with him
also freely give us all things?*

God says, "I want you to love me genuinely and
consistently; sacrificially and unconditionally. Don't
just love Me when it's convenient, but also when it is not
so convenient." What about when you encounter great
persecution; when your reputation is on the line? Can we
love endlessly? What about giving up all those little, no harm
things that hinder our relationship with the Lord? Can we
freely walk away from all and trust Him to never allow us to
be embarrassed or put to shame? Can we honestly trust Him

for abundant provision? When we can say, "He means more to us than life itself and live this way, then and only then have we truly surrendered to Him." A life totally yielded to God says, "whatever you want to do Lord, I am available to follow. I purpose in my heart to submit to you, resist the devil and lay aside anything that would keep me from being all you have called me to be."

James 4:7

Submit yourselves therefore to God. Resist the devil, and he will flee from you. Draw nigh to God, and He will draw nigh to you.... (No man can resist the devil unless he first submits to God).

Hebrews 12:1-2

Wherefore seeing we also are compassed about with so great a cloud of witnesses, let us lay aside every weight, and the sin which doth so easily beset us, and let us run with patience the race that is set before us, looking unto Jesus the author and finisher of our faith; who for the joy that was set before him endured the cross, despising the shame, and is set down at the right hand of the throne of God.

If there is no enemy within; there is no enemy without great enough to defeat us. Herein lies the truth; the enemy defeating us, lives within us, and it is not what happens to us that determines victory or defeat, but how we respond to what is happening to us; how we respond is based upon where we are in our thoughts. Yieldedness to God will prompt us to monitor the thoughts of our minds and bring every thought subject to the law of God.

Isaiah 64:4
For since the beginning of the world men have not heard, nor perceived by the ear neither hath the eye seen, O God, beside thee, what he hath prepared for him that waiteth for him.

God wants us to wait on Him in order that He may unfold His perfect will. He fashions us as He has planned and calls us to wait **in His presence**. Something awesome happens when we wait **in the presence of God**. I speak of things I have literally experienced. I have experienced a transformation in my very personality while waiting before God. There is just something about being silent in the presence of God. A holy calm is bestowed upon us. We don't want to move. Every part of our being is saturated with His presence. We don't want to say a word. All we want to do is enjoy His glory. The deep need for this waiting on God lies equally in the nature of every born-again believer. God, as Creator, formed man to be a vessel through which He could show forth His power and goodness.

Lamentations 3:26
It is good that a man should both hope and quietly wait for the salvation of the Lord.

The Bible tells us to take heed, and be quiet. It tells us to fear not, neither be faint-hearted. In quietness before God, and in confidence in God, we find strength. These words display the close connection between quietness and faith. God reveals what a deep need there is for quietness, as an element of true waiting on God. If we are to have our whole heart turned towards God, we must have it turned away from all created things, from all that occupies our time and holds our interests, whether they inspire happiness or sorrow. The very thought of God, in His majesty and holiness should silence us. Over and over the scriptures tell of this truth.

Habakkuk 2:20
The Lord is in his holy temple: let all the earth keep silence before Him.

Zephaniah 1:7
Hold thy peace at the presence of God.

Zechariah 2:13
Be silent, O all flesh before the Lord: for He is raised up out of his holy habitation.

Waiting on God is comprised of watchful expectation, yieldedness and stillness (which is quietness and respectful reverence). **In His Presence** there is a time to speak, a time to listen, and a time to be quiet before God. As long as waiting on God is primarily thought of as a step toward more productive prayer, and answers to one's requests alone, the spirit of perfect quietness will not be obtained. But when waiting on God is itself seen as an unsurpassed blessing, one of the highest forms of fellowship with the Holy One, the adoration of Him in His glory, then it will consequently humble the soul into a holy stillness, making the way open for God to speak and reveal Himself.

If believers are to master the art of waiting on God, it is imperative to learn to quietly wait, by taking time to be away from all friends, all duties, all cares, and all joys. We must take time to be still before God, not only to acquire stillness from man and the world, but from self and its energies. We must let the Word of God and prayer have pre-eminence. Prayer and study of the Word will admonish us, when it is time to be still and wait before God. There are times when God calls us aside to just listen to Him. There have been times in my own life when I would plan to go before God and pray for a list of people, situations and/or circumstances. God would simply move upon me gently to worship Him. There have been times when I'd go into the Father's presence to worship Him and He would gently lead me to be silent. On other occasions I have entered His presence to pray in my native language (English) and He leads me to just pray in the Spirit (prayer in tongues).

Whichever way He leads, I follow. Why? Because it is in following His leadership that I enjoy His fullness. Often we want to do it our way and enter God's presence with a set structure. We must remember that communion with God is two-way. We must allow God to direct our time with Him. When we are yielded to God, He can gently lead us as He wills. There are even times when He initiates our times of communion. He may gently awaken you at two or three in the morning. You will know when it's His call for you to come aside and dine with Him. Nothing brings peace and satisfaction like what you experience **in His presence**, in the wee hours of the morning. Just yield to Him, for, it is then that we experience inner peace and fulfillment that literally overwhelms us as we achieve great success in all walks of life. You see, His direction is perfect. We just surrender our way, for His way. His way is perfect and brings illumination; not just concerning spiritual things but in every area of our lives.

When you and I value our time with God, we'll began to value ourselves, as we see ourselves in light of the truth. Until we value our time **in His Presence**, we will not value ourselves, for we will never come to know who we truly are apart from **His presence**. If we do not value time with God, we will never walk in light of God's best in the fullness He has for us. Our values are the foundational building blocks of our character and confidence. A person who does not know what he stands for or what he should stand for will not enjoy true happiness and success. True happiness and success comes from knowing God, as our Father and who He has fashioned us to be. We belong to the everlasting God Jehovah. Jehovah means self-existing one; having no origin; "complete." Therefore, we are complete in Him.

Chapter Seven

Excellence of Spirit

*E*xcellence of Spirit reveals the condition of one's heart. God looks on the inside. What a man is on the outside is a direct reflection of what he is within. God examines the inside; this is why David said in **Psalm 139:23-24** *"Search me, O God, and know my heart: try me, and know my thoughts: and see if there be any wicked way in me, and lead me in the way everlasting."*

Excellence of spirit portrays itself by excelling the usual. It is the condition of the heart that enables us to possess an unusually high quality of integrity, ethics and character. The heart tells if we are superior in quality and outstanding in measure. In these last days, when the integrity and character of the believer is questioned as never before, an excellent spirit is extremely important. Especially since we, as God's representatives, must live as an open book before all men in a manner that is above reproach. We must purpose in our hearts at all times to be mindful of who we are, and never yield to anything that will bring shame or embarrassment on the Body of Christ.

Proverbs 16:1-7

The preparations of the heart (the soul) in man, and the answer of the tongue, is from the Lord. All the ways of a man are clean in his own eyes: but the Lord weigheth the

*spirits. Commit thy works unto the Lord, and
thy thoughts shall be established. The Lord
hath made all things for himself: yea, even
the wicked for the day of evil. Every one that
is proud in heart is an abomination to the
Lord: though hand join in hand, he shall not
be unpunished. By mercy and truth iniquity
is purged: and by the fear of the Lord men
depart from evil. When a man's ways please
the Lord, he maketh even his enemies to be at
peace with him.*

An excellent spirit is established when a man
commits his way to the Lord. The Bible speaks of the eyes
of the Lord running to and fro throughout the whole earth;
He is searching the earth for people who are committed. He
looks for those whose hearts are pure and undefiled before
Him. God wants to show Himself strong on the behalf of
those who trust in Him with their whole heart. He longs to
display His power and magnificence on the behalf of those
who possess an excellent spirit. God looks for pure motive
of heart, which will trigger the release of pure actions.

II Chronicles 16:9
*For the eyes of the Lord run to and fro
throughout the whole earth, to shew himself
strong in the behalf of them whose heart is
perfect toward him....*

Hebrews 4:13
*Neither is there any creature that is not
manifest in his sight: but all things are naked
and opened unto the eyes of him with whom
we have to do.*

As we examine excellence of spirit, I want to share the following words God spoke to my spirit:

> *"My people worship Me after form and not after the heart; for they know not the God that I am. As much as I have revealed Myself in My Word, it has not become a reality in the hearts of the people. Are you so cold at heart that you cannot discern my nature, nor my love? For surely if you will know Me after the spirit, in blessing, I will bless you. Said I not, that I am the God that changes not, even from days of old, I am the same eternally. I see into the depths of your hearts and I know your every thought. I would, that you would know Me, even as I know and love you, for I am your Father, I am alive forever, and I show mercy to thousands who love Me and honor Me. I desire the deepest worship from the heart and not in ceremony. Surely I desire truth in the inward parts. Would you come higher, says the Lord; would you come higher? Walk with Me, and I will ever walk with you. Your dependence on Me now is shallow, but if you seek Me with your whole heart and turn your face only towards Me, surely you will experience My tender loving care and My power in a dimension you never thought possible. I will elevate you and cause you to experience a fullness in My presence that is rarely experienced, because many will not come aside and taste of this great thing, I have prepared for those who will walk with Me."*

God looks at what is in the heart of man (the soul). Why? The answer is found in **Proverbs 4:23** which says, *"Keep thy heart with all diligence; for out of it are the issues of life."* God says the soul of man is saturated with the components that structure his life. He says we should guard our hearts. How is this done? Our spirit is guarded as we control what we see, what we say and what we hear. Information gets into our spirit by what we see, say, and hear. God is concerned with the condition of man's soul. Whatever man is within, is revealed in his life. Jesus said in **Matthew 15:17-20**, *"Do not ye yet understand, that whatsoever entereth in at the mouth goeth into the belly, and is cast out into the draught (sewer)? But those things which proceed out of the mouth come forth from the heart; and they defile the man. For out of the heart proceed evil thoughts, murders, adulteries, fornications, thefts, false witness, blasphemies: these are the things which defile a man: but to eat with unwashen hands defileth not a man."*

Our relationship with our heavenly Father must be valued above all else. As we develop our relationship with Him we experience a daily transformation. We will not allow ourselves to be contaminated by watching everything the world puts before us in the way of the filth exposed on television, movies, magazines, etc. The spirit of man in the scriptures above, refers to the soul-heart; the seat of the man's mind, will, emotions, desires, intellect, imagination, and reasoning.

Let me mention, that, television is one of the most powerful vehicles used by the forces of darkness to influence and corrupt the thinking of mankind. Much of the time spent watching filthy, profane movies can be used as time to develop one's relationship with the Lord by prayer and study of God's Word. Watching television appeases the flesh and many refuse to turn away from it for God. Just as sure as we put it before our eyes, it will affect the condition of our hearts. I am not saying it is wrong to watch a good wholesome television program. I am saying television should not consume us; and we must be particular regarding our choice of movies.

God spoke these words to me sharply, when I was consumed with watching television. He said, *"I have called you for a great and a mighty work, you must separate yourself from anything that will rob you of time spent in My presence and in My Word."* I am not saying that to watch television is wrong. Television is also a powerful vehicle to carry the gospel. I am simply saying if you spend more time in front of television than you do in prayer, or in the Word, you need to make some adjustments in your life, and consider what is of the greatest value to you.

Much of what is shown on television today is filled with violence, sexual perversion, abuse, profanity, and gross wickedness. Our soul is much too sensitive to be exposed to that which defiles and contaminates. All of the above, defile and contaminate and will keep us from possessing excellence in spirit. A person is not born with excellence of Spirit. Excellence of Spirit originates directly from one's commitment to God, and relationship with God. Excellence of Spirit is rooted and grounded in the heart as a direct result of man's deliberate pursuit of God's Word and his eagerness to sow that Word into the heart. Man establishes the course of his life by speaking God's Word and living in absolute agreement with God's Word as exemplified in moral excellence and integrity.

A few of the key components that cause one to develop an excellent spirit are:

1) attention to the Word of God;
2) application of the Word of God;
3) deposition of the Word in the heart by meditation and speaking;
4) refusal to have a froward mouth or a conversation void of the truth of God's Word; and,
5) a consistent, disciplined time of fellowship and communion with God.

Proverbs 4:20-27

My son, <u>attend</u> to my words; incline thine ear unto my sayings. Let them not depart from thine eyes; keep them in the midst of thine heart. For they are life unto those that find them, and health to all their flesh. Keep thy heart (soul) with all diligence; for out of it are the issues of life. Put away from thee a froward mouth, and perverse lips put far from thee. Let thine eyes look right on, and let thine eyelids look straight before thee. Ponder the path of thy feet, and let all thy ways be established. Turn not to the right hand nor to the left: remove thy foot from evil.

God looks for those who are pure in heart and excellent in spirit (excellent in soul). There is a man in scripture that had a reputation for being one who had such a spirit.

Daniel 6:3

Then this Daniel was preferred above the presidents and princes, because an excellent

*spirit was in him; and the king thought to set
him over the whole realm.*

Daniel, whose name means God is Judge, had a
reputation for being one who could solve hard sentences.
He could interpret dreams and dissolve doubts. The Bible
says he had an excellent spirit, was full of knowledge, had
great understanding and the Holy Spirit. Can you see other
components of an excellent spirit? How did Daniel acquire
an excellent spirit? We have shared the answer all throughout
this book. Daniel was a man committed to prayer. Any person
who genuinely conforms to the ways of God will possess an
excellent spirit. Why? Our Father has an excellent spirit. We
can have no less when we are truly committed to Him. The
key to Daniel possessing an excellent spirit is clearly revealed
in **Daniel 6:4-5**, *"Then the presidents and princes sought to
find occasion against Daniel concerning the kingdom; but
they could find none occasion or fault; for as much as he was
faithful, neither was there any error or fault found in him.
Then said these men, we shall not find any occasion against
this Daniel, except we find it against him concerning the law
of his God."*

Other components of an excellent spirit are **steadfastness**,
faithfulness, **integrity**, **character** and **sinlessness**.
Sinlessness simply refers to the world's inability to find fault
in the righteous. It does not mean the righteous will never
make a mistake. It simply refers to a lifestyle committed
to moral excellence. It refers to one's commitment to live
holy before all men and abstain from the appearance of evil.
Excellence in spirit is the cornerstone for character. Character
is the ability to carry out a worthy decision after the emotion
of making that decision has passed. It is not an attribute one
is born with, nor the result of being born into the family of

God. Character is developed as man develops his relationship with God and commits to live in the ways of God, despite persecution or temptation. Integrity is a man's complete adherence to the Word of God without compromise. It is his commitment, not only to God, but to himself as one who can be trusted in all facets of life, regardless of circumstances.

Daniel lived by certain laws that governed his personal productivity, human relationships, his relationship with God, and personal achievements. These laws dramatically affected the course of his life. He experienced promotion, God's protective and delivering power, and fulfillment as a man of God, no matter what opposition he faced.

Excellence of spirit makes things happen. It causes one to plan, by seeking out solutions, never leaning on excuses. Excellence of Spirit recognizes the need for change and does not procrastinate because of obstacles but forges ahead. Excellence of spirit compels one to work at being better. It commands respect and will never compromise or back down during a challenge. Excellence of Spirit says, "I'll do what it takes to receive maximum results." Excellence of Spirit generates high productivity, high self esteem, and confidence in a faithful God. **It seeks excellence, yet serves others**. It is wise, yet compassionate. It is humble and honest, bold and confident. It is generous, focused, and sound. Competent, yet teachable. It is secure, reliable, and dependable. Excellence of Spirit dares to step outside of one's comfort zone to achieve even greater dimensions of spiritual growth. It boldly speaks the Word of God, understanding that faith declares what is not seen, bringing what is not seen into the present. Excellence of spirit enables one to have a clearer view of what the ideal future looks like. It does not yield to procrastination which is described as follows:

"Procrastination is a close relative of incompetence and a handmaiden of inefficiency."

Every child of God can have excellence of spirit if they are willing to be true to God, commit all to God, and purpose to achieve nothing less than God's best in every area of life. The Bible says, Daniel was a man in whom there was no blemish, but he was well favored, and skillful in all wisdom, and cunning in knowledge and understanding science, and had the ability to stand in the King's palace **(Daniel 1:4)**. The following scriptures will further reveal why Daniel was acknowledged as one having an excellent spirit:

Daniel was not a man of compromise:

Daniel 1:8

But Daniel purposed in his heart that he would not defile himself with the portion of the kings's meat, nor with the wine which he drank: therefore he requested of the prince of the eunuchs that he might not defile himself.

Daniel was a man of wisdom and understanding, yet he was always dependent on God:

Daniel 1:20

And in all matters of wisdom and understanding, that the king inquired of them, he found them ten times better than all the magicians and astrologers that were in all his realm.

Daniel 2:19-23

Then was the secret revealed unto Daniel in a night vision. Then Daniel blessed the God of heaven. Daniel answered and said, blessed be the name of God for ever and ever; for wisdom and might are his: and he changeth the times and the seasons; he removeth kings, and setteth up kings: he giveth wisdom unto the wise, and knowledge to them that know understanding: he revealeth the deep and secret things: he knoweth what is in the darkness, and the light dwelleth with him. I thank thee, and praise thee, O thou God of my fathers, who hast given me wisdom and might, and hast made known unto me now what we desired of thee: for thou hast now made known unto us the king's matter.

Daniel 5:13-14

Then was Daniel brought in before the king. And the king spake and said unto Daniel, art thou that Daniel, which are of the children of the captivity of Judah, whom the king my father brought out of Jewry? I have even heard of thee, that the spirit of the gods is in thee, and that light and understanding and excellent wisdom is found in thee.

Daniel was a man committed to prayer:

Daniel 6:10

Now when Daniel knew that the writing was signed, he went into his house; and his window being open in his chamber toward

Jerusalem, he kneeled upon his knees three times a day, and prayed and gave thanks before his God as he did aforetime.

I have included these scriptures because here we find the ingredients of excellence in spirit and how Daniel acquired such a spirit. ***Daniel would not compromise. He served God faithfully for 80 to 90 years. God promoted him, and gave him wisdom in all the affairs of life. Daniel stayed in the presence of God, and no matter how he was promoted in life, he never failed to bless the Lord and rely upon Him***. If we will possess excellence in spirit, all that we see in Daniel should be in us. It should be visible.

How does one develop excellence of spirit? First of all an individual must be committed to God. He must hunger and thirst for excellence in all things and dare to rise above the most subtle form of deception and compromise. Excellence breeds conformity to a righteous standard. This standard is the Word of God. It is what we often refer to as virtue. Virtue comes from a Hebrew word, "chayil," which means strong in all moral and mental qualities. Virtue is the backbone of man's power source, for we will never walk in the fullness of the power of God without virtuous living.

We must abide in the Word of God and allow the Word of God to abide in us. This simply means, God's Word dictates what we do, what we say, where we go, what we think, how we view our selves, and how we view others. We purpose in our hearts to honor our word, even as our Father honors His Word and we always refuse to glory in ourselves, but rather in the power of God.

111

What is an Excellent Spirit? Excellence comes from the Hebrew word "yattiyr" (yat-teer) and means greatness; exceptional; of a higher nature or kind than others; of great value; revealing an attitude of being above average; superior; prime; transcending the negative, normal, and mediocre; to pass beyond what is expected of average people; the visible essence of inward greatness; living above and independent of negative people, circumstances, difficulties, and resistance.

Excellence also comes from the Greek word "huperbole" and means a throwing beyond; a surpassing; exceeding greatness; beyond measure; the ability to reach one's highest potential. Excellence of Spirit refers to brilliance of mind (soul), such that whatever one sets his will to accomplish, God will honor and empower him to succeed. Excellence of Spirit says, every thought pattern has been tested, examined, measured by the Word of God and submitted to the Word of God. The Bible says, Daniel was a man of knowledge and understanding. He was brilliant.

Brilliant means unusually keen and alert in mind; distinguished as a high achiever; outstandingly successful; a man of discernment and wisdom. A man who made God clear and visible in his mind, such that his external behavior revealed his thoughts made visible.

Man's behavior is rooted in man's thoughts and not his spirit. Our thoughts are directing the course of our lives for good or for evil. What kinds of thoughts do you have? The thoughts of our minds will tell us how close we are to God, or how far away from God we really are. How did Daniel become a man of such brilliance? Daniel was a man of prayer. He made his goal in life, his chief aim in life, to please God. He had a mind to make God clear and visible.

Daniel was a man who was able to show forth stability and wisdom in changing circumstances. In captivity, the Babylonians tried to change his identity. An excellent spirit will enable us to overcome negative situations and circumstances without harm; without setbacks.

An excellent spirit will not allow us to waddle in despair, self-pity, grief, or depression. An excellent spirit causes us to rise above the challenges of life. Why? We see challenges as opportunities for God to glorify Himself and show forth His greatness as God. We see obstacles as a means by which to perfect us and not destroy us.

An excellent spirit is like an alarm system. When down thoughts come, defeated thoughts come, failure thoughts come, an excellent spirit sounds an alarm, warning us that a thief is trespassing in an attempt to steal, kill and destroy; an intruder is lurking about with one mission in mind, to destroy.

Daniel was a man of self-discipline.

Daniel whose name means (God is Judge); knew who he was.

He would not defile himself for the sake of pleasing man or his flesh.

He would not conform to the world.

Daniel was not ashamed of his God.

Daniel did not fear dying for who he was and what he believed.

Daniel was a man of fervent and consistent prayer.

Daniel had:

1. Knowledge -   a relationship with truth, such that he would not make a move without searching the heart of God. He lived in a constant oneness with truth.

2. Discipline -   soundness and safety of mind; behavior trained and developed by instruction and correction; control acquired through consistent obedience; conduct ordered by truth; enforced submission to truth.

3. Understanding -   a mind brought under the correct interpretation of knowledge; discernment as a result of a mind yielded to God; to hold truth in the mind; if a man does not hold truth in his mind; he will sin against God.

4. Wisdom -   ability to apply knowledge with conviction at the proper time in the proper place regardless to the people present or the surrounding conditions.

5. Boldness -   void of fear of man.

6. Steadfastness -   unable to be persuaded to move against God; seated in peace; firmly settled without doubt; void of a bent toward moving.

7. Prayer -   communion with God.

When a believer accepts God's Word as truth, that believer is saying that he or she assumes full responsibility for what they heard and received as true, to the point of rearranging their entire life to enter in agreement with the truth.

To "accept" means one is willing to receive, as true, by a deliberate and ready reception, what is offered without protest. Truth accepted must become visible. If one refuses to accept the truth of God's Word, the growth and development of that individual is hindered.

If one's growth is hindered, then the perfect will of God for one's life is in jeopardy. No believer should remain the same as God's Word is being introduced to us. Growth for the believer should be an ongoing occurrence. No man can do all God has called him to do in an immature state.

Growth is a steady progression towards full-development. God will not require anything of us that He has not already equipped us to handle.

Daniel already knew what we must come into the knowledge of. With God, we have greatness within us. We have untapped potential. We are born of the incorruptible seed of the Word of God that liveth and abideth forever.

I Peter 1:22-23
Seeing ye have purified your souls in obeying the truth through the Spirit unto unfeigned love of the brethren, see that ye love one another with a pure heart fervently: Being born again, not of corruptible seed, but of incorruptible, by the Word of God, which liveth and abideth forever.

The seed of greatness is in you and in me; the seed of excellence; the seed of unlimited power. God's Word is seed and is preprogrammed to produce after its own kind. We have the capacity to expose the excellence God has made available to us.

Teaching will produce change in those who are willing to pay the price. You and I will change when, in our own minds, the benefits of change are greater than the pain of not changing. All change involves pain, but the benefit of change is greater than the pain.

Change in God is not a temporary adjustment, but rather a complete overhaul. A metamorphosis; a shedding; a putting off of the old and putting on of the new. Everyday, we live, we can either choose to be a victim or we can choose to live life victoriously. We can choose to serve God or satan. We can choose life or death. We can choose to be negative or think out of the mind of God. We can choose to get up and make things happen or we can choose to mope around and wait on things to happen. We can choose to believe in ourselves and work hard to advance ourselves or we can die broke, miserable, sick, depressed, whining, blaming others, criticizing, never having made a difference in life.

We're created to win. We were born to win, but we have been conditioned to lose. Ninety percent (90%) of what we hear and speak is negative. We wake up expecting the negative. We think the negative. We speak negatively. We even surround ourselves with negative people, negative movies, and negative music. We are programmed with the negative. We cannot develop excellence of spirit if we surround ourselves with negativity.

New Years' Resolutions are emotional decisions. Many of us made them and here we are halfway through the first month of the year and we have failed to implement a plan.

God wants us to put this new life in Him on display. He wants this life we have in Him to be magnified and highlighted. He wants us to boast of His goodness. He wants us to sing aloud of His greatness. He wants to be magnified so the heathen will be jealous of our life in Him and desire what we have over what they have.

That's why He said; You are the salt of the earth.

Matthew 5:13-16

Ye are the salt of the earth; but if the salt have lost his savor wherewith shall it be salted? It is thenceforth good for nothing, but to be cast out, and to be trodden under foot of men. Ye are the light of the world. A city that is set on a hill cannot be hid. Neither do men light a candle, and put it under a bushel, but on a candlestick; and it giveth light unto all that are in the house. Let your light so shine before men, that they may see your good works, and glorify your Father, which is in heaven.

Salt is abundant in nature and is used for:

1. A cure - to restore health; soundness; to bring out of spiritual ruin; to bring out of an unhealthy or undesirable state.
2. To make rich by adding value.
3. To flavor or give life to; add sharpness and wit.
4. Season - make fit for use; fit for serving.
5. Preserve - to keep safe from harm or destruction.
6. Purify - to free from impurities, corruption, toxins, polluting or damaging elements; to make pure and clean.
7. Salt exposes what is hidden.

We are the light so that the blind might receive their sight (make increase through witnessing).

Matthew 4:16

The people which sat in darkness saw great light; and to them which sat in theregion and shadow of death light is sprung up.

You are the light of the world. The world has constantly put its sin in our face. Instead of us holding up the light and bragging in God, we shame the name by getting in bed with the world; as if the pleasures of sin have a greater value than new life in God.

Daniel's name once again means "God is Judge" and his name is certainly in harmony with his beliefs, convictions, and his behavior. Daniel was a man who was familiar with change. But there is one element that kept Daniel steady during seasons of change. Daniel had an excellent spirit. ("Spirit" in **Daniel 6:3,** comes from the Hebrew word "Ruach" and means mind).

Daniel was a spiritually dead man. Therefore, when the Bible says he was a man with an "**Excellent Spirit**", the scripture was not referring to his inner man, but rather, his soul; his mind; his attitude.

You and I can develop an excellent spirit and truly be the salt of the earth, if we are willing to commune with God in prayer and allow Him to shape us into vessels of honor fit for the Master's use. We can exercise the power of our will to think correctly, and we can change our entire lives if we are willing to renew our minds.

118

Romans 12:1-3

I beseech you therefore, brethren, by the mercies of God, that ye present your bodies a living sacrifice, holy, acceptable unto God, which is your reasonable service. And be not conformed to this world: but be ye transformed by the renewing of your mind, that ye may prove what is that good, and acceptable, and perfect, will of God. For I say, through the grace given unto me, to every man that is among you, not to think of himself more highly than he ought to think; but to think soberly, according as God hath dealt to every man the measure of faith.

Walking in the Spirit

Galatians 5:16-17

This I say then, walk in the Spirit, and ye shall not fulfill the lust of the flesh. For the flesh lusteth against the Spirit, and the Spirit against the flesh: and these are contrary the one to the other: so that ye cannot do the things that ye would.

One of the greatest keys to abiding **in the Presence of God** is walking in the Spirit. This is a phrase used often, but not explicitly understood. What does it mean to walk in the spirit? First of all "walk" refers to the pursuit of a course of action or manner of living. It refers to a lifestyle in which believers purposefully pursue a lifestyle totally ordered or ruled by the Word of God. The believer chooses to consistently be a doer of the Word no matter what the circumstance. To walk in the Spirit does not carry the appearance of one who is spooky or weird, but simply denotes behavior that exemplifies the character of God. This type of living requires discipline and discipline is the act of training the soul to respond to God by renewing the mind with God's Word daily and controlling the flesh. Discipline is training that corrects, molds and perfects the believer. A disciplined lifestyle is accomplished by enforcing obedience. It is the act of self-control, wherein obedience to God becomes more important than the cravings of the body and soul. Walking in the spirit refers to a constant awareness of the presence of God and the ability to respond to the Father's presence at any given moment.

Romans 8:6-13

For to be carnally minded is death; but to be spiritually minded is life and peace. Because the carnal mind is enmity against God: for it is not subject to the law of God, neither indeed can be. So then they that are in the flesh cannot please God. But ye are not in the flesh, but in the Spirit, if so be that the Spirit of God dwell in you. Now if any man have not the Spirit of Christ, he is none of his. And if Christ be in you the body is dead because of sin; but the Spirit is life because of righteousness. But if the Sprit of him that raised up Jesus from the dead dwell in you, he that raised up Jesus from the dead shall also quicken your mortal bodies by his Spirit that dwelleth in you. Therefore, brethren, we are debtors, not to the flesh, to live after the flesh. For if ye live after the flesh, ye shall die: but if ye through the Spirit do mortify the deeds of the body, ye shall live.

The only way to overcome temptation and lusts of the flesh is to walk in the Spirit. God calls us to live habitually in the Spirit. He speaks of us living our lives totally responsive to the Spirit of God who lives within us. If we are ever conscious of the indwelling power of God and are willing to discipline ourselves to respond to the presence of God within, we can live a victorious life over the lusts of the flesh. We must develop a hatred for sin and renounce the works of the flesh. The works of the flesh include adultery, uncleanness, lasciviousness (which is the promoting or partaking of that which tends to produce lewd emotions; anything tending to foster sex sins and lust), idolatry, witchcraft, hatred, dissensions, or discord, envy, jealousy, murder, the list goes on. Let me encourage the believer, by saying we can live above the temptations of the flesh. Temptations will come, but we make the decision ultimately whether or not to yield; even as we make the decision to yield to God. The forces of evil cannot force a man to sin. A man sins of his own free will. God respects our right to choose. He simply admonishes us to choose good. You and I are where we are today because of choices we have made.

James 1:12-16
Blessed is the man that endureth temptation: for when he is tried, he shall receive the crown of life, which the Lord hath promised to them that love him. Let no man say when he is tempted, I am tempted of God: for God cannot be tempted with evil, neither tempteth he any man: but every man is tempted when he is drawn away of his own lust, and enticed. Then when lust hath conceived, it bringeth forth sin: and sin, when it is finished, bringeth forth death (separation from God). Do not err, my beloved brethren.

Deuteronomy 30:19
I call heaven and earth to record this day against you, that I have set before you life and death, blessing and cursing: therefore choose life, that both thou and thy seed may live:

To walk in the Spirit requires effort and is not easily attained. Let's examine key scriptures that reveal how this walk in the spirit is attained.

Colossians 3:1-3
If ye then be risen with Christ, <u>seek those things which are above, where Christ sitteth on the right hand of God. Set your affection on things above, not on things on the earth.</u> For ye are dead, and your life is hid with Christ in God.

Colossians 3:5-10
<u>Mortify therefore your members which are upon the earth;</u> fornication, uncleanness, inordinate affection, evil concupiscence, and covetousness, which is idolatry: For which things' sake the wrath of God cometh on the children of disobedience: In the which ye also walked some time, when ye lived in them. But now ye also put off all these; anger, wrath, malice, blasphemy, filthy communication out of your mouth. Lie not one to another, seeing that ye have put off the old man with his deeds; And have put on the new man, which is renewed in knowledge after the image of him that created him:

The Apostle Paul, in his writing to the church at Colosse, as inspired by the Holy Spirit, admonishes believers that because they are born again they must search diligently for those things that are beneficial to developing a closer relationship with God. He tells them that they can no longer trust in the things that are subject to corruption, subject to decay; but they must embrace those things that cannot be destroyed. He further explains that they are dead to the old nature and alive to God. Spiritual maturity is not acquired by osmosis, but through a process of training oneself and demanding growth of oneself by study of God's Word, prayer, and application of God's Word. I would like to emphasize that knowledge does not bring freedom in life. It is the application of the knowledge acquired that brings freedom and freedom promotes spiritual growth.

Paul says, "Don't base life's success on this world's system which is subject to fail." There is nothing wrong with a college education, wealth, a beautiful home, automobile, etc. However, man's chief objective should not be to amass great materialistic wealth. Man's total affection should not be focused on the accumulation of wealth or secular achievements. His paramount objective should be developing his relationship with God.

Luke 12:15
And he said unto them, take heed, and beware of covetousness: for a man's life consisteth not in the abundance of the things which he possesseth.

Matthew 6:19-21
Lay not up for yourselves treasures upon earth, where moth and rust doth corrupt, and where thieves break through and steal: but lay up for yourselves treasures in heaven, where neither moth nor rust doth corrupt, and where thieves do not break through nor steal: For where your treasure is, there will your heart be also.

125

To walk in the Spirit requires clear focus and all things put in proper perspective. God wants his children to enjoy the best. However, He requires that we love Him more than the benefits He provides. He requires that we love Him, not for what He can give, but because of who He is. This issue must be settled in the heart and mind of every believer who desires to walk in the Spirit.

We have been placed in the same class with God. We are spirit (**I Thessalonians 5:23**) as we have discussed in Chapter 1, and are free to worship God in Spirit and in Truth, every second of our lives. We touch God because He is Spirit (**John 4:24**). To live in God's presence enables us to live in the spirit. What does it mean to live in the spirit? Living in the Spirit causes man to be more spirit-led than sense ruled. It causes men to be ever conscious of God and less affected by circumstances. Living in the Spirit simply means we allow God's Word to dictate our attitude, what we do, what we say, where we go, and who we establish relationships with.

II Corinthians 6:16-17

And what agreement hath the temple of God with idols? For ye are the temple of the living God; as God hath said, I will dwell in them, and walk in them; and I will be their God and they shall be my people. Wherefore come out from among them, and be ye separate, saith the Lord, and touch not the unclean thing: and I will receive you. And will be a Father unto you, and ye shall be my sons and daughters, saith the Lord Almighty.

God makes it clear, if we will seek first the kingdom, and his righteousness; all things required for living a good life on planet earth will be provided. What does it mean to seek first the Kingdom of God? This statement means to eagerly acknowledge the rulership of God in the earth through born again men. God rules in this earth through His body. His kingdom cannot be established in this earth without every believer allowing Him to operate in planet earth through them. God's righteousness is established in the earth as born again men exemplify the power of God by living before others free of greed and lust. The born again believer represents the righteousness of God in the earth.

Matthew 6:33
But seek ye first the kingdom of God, and his righteousness; and all these things shall be added unto you.

To walk in the Spirit demands self-control. A man can not live a spirit-led life if he is constantly concerned about appeasing the flesh.

Ephesians 4:17-32
This I say therefore, and testify in the Lord, that ye henceforth walk not as other Gentiles walk, in the vanity of their mind, Having the understanding darkened, being alienated from the life of God through the ignorance that is in them, because of the blindness of their heart: Who being past feeling have given themselves over unto lasciviousness, to work all uncleanness with greediness. But ye have not so learned Christ; If so be that ye have heard him, and have been taught by him, as the truth is in Jesus: That ye put off concerning the former conversation

127

*the old man, which is corrupt according
to the deceitful lusts; And be renewed in
the spirit of your mind; And that ye put on
the new man, which after God is created in
righteousness and true holiness. Wherefore
putting away lying, speak every man truth
with his neighbour: for we are members one
of another. Be ye angry, and sin not: let not
the sun go down upon your wrath: Neither
give place to the devil. Let him that stole steal
no more: but rather let him labour, working
with his hands the thing which is good, that
he may have to give to him that needeth. Let
no corrupt communication proceed out of
your mouth, but that which is good to the use
of edifying, that it may minister grace unto
the hearers. And grieve not the holy Spirit of
God, whereby ye are sealed unto the day of
redemption. Let all bitterness, and wrath, and
anger, and clamour, and evil speaking, be put
away from you, with all malice: And be ye
kind one to another, tenderhearted, forgiving
one another, even as God for Christ's sake
hath forgiven you.*

The conditions of walking in the Spirit are concise and
always bring reward. Man must simply exercise the power
of his will to obey God.

I Corinthians 9:24-27
*Know ye not that they which run in a race run
all, but one receiveth the prize? So run, that
ye may obtain. And every man that striveth
for the mastery is temperate in all things.*

*Now they do it to obtain a corruptible crown;
but we an incorruptible. I therefore so run,
not as uncertainly; so fight I, not as one that
beateth the air: But I keep under my body,
and bring it into subjection: lest that by any
means, when I have preached to others, I
myself should be a castaway.*

We cannot go through life aimlessly expecting to experience the power of God in a great measure if our lives are not consecrated before God. We must demand excellence of ourselves, literally control the thoughts of our minds, control our bodies and seek God's standard for living, which is not erroneous nor fanatical, but perfect and plainly outlined in the Bible. There is no room for misunderstanding because God has vowed if we receive His words, He will give understanding unto the simple.

Psalm 119:130
*The entrance of thy words giveth light; it
giveth understanding unto the simple.*

Psalm 119:133
*Order my steps in thy word: and let not any
iniquity have dominion over me.*

Every believer who desires to walk in the Spirit, must long to please God and seek His face. We must understand that God is not in the business of recruiting spooky or flaky people. To walk in the Spirit does not mean we float through life with our heads in the clouds. As a matter of truth, those who walk in the spirit are usually humble, submitted to authority, and very wise. They are extremely keen in spiritual things. They are people who are balanced in the Word of

God and submitted to God. They are not loud and unseemly in behavior, but meek in spirit, yet bold in the things of God. They are not spotlight people, but rather those who prefer to sit in the background and listen to the voice of God while serving others. When it is time to speak, all those who listen and hear will know they walk with God. Those who walk in the spirit, to put it simply, are those who walk with God.

All believers must decide to yield to God by training the flesh to come subject to the appetite of the re-created spirit of man. When spiritual things become more important than all else, then and only then can we enjoy the benefits of ***walking in the spirit***.

The sum total of walking in the spirit is an ever conscious awareness of the presence of God, dependence on His presence, yieldedness to His presence, and a heart that responds to His presence, without always understanding His leading.

Galatians 2:20

I am crucified with Christ: nevertheless I live; yet not I, but Christ liveth in me: and the life which I now live in the flesh I live by the faith of the Son of God, who loved me, and gave himself for me.

Chapter Nine

Ministering to the Lord

Psalm 100:1-5

*Make a joyful noise unto the Lord, all ye lands.
Serve the Lord with gladness: come before
His presence with singing. Know ye that the
Lord he is God: it is he that hath made us, and
not we ourselves; we are his people, and the
sheep of his pasture. Enter into his gates with
thanksgiving, and into his courts with praise:
be thankful unto him, and bless his name. For
the Lord is good; his mercy is everlasting and
his truth endureth to all generations.*

There is something awesome that happens during a time of praise and worship. The manifestation of God's power is felt in praise and worship. I believe praise and worship exemplifies the total essence of faith in God and invokes supernatural things to happen as we take the time just to minister to the Lord. Praise and Worship is the highest form of prayer, simply because it pleases the Father to know we can adore Him even in the most difficult times. It rejoices His heart when we worship Him not for what He can and will do, but because of who He is and because of what He has already done.

Anybody can praise God when everything is going well in life. It takes faith in God to worship Him in the darkest of

131

days, when we see no way out; it was during such a time as this when Paul and Silas were bound in jail (**Acts 16:16-34**). They were committed to God and while fulfilling the call of God on their lives, they encountered great persecution. As they were bound in jail on one occasion, their backs bleeding from being beaten and their feet were in stocks, they made a decision to worship God. There is much significance to their feet being in stocks. These Roman stocks were not only made to keep them from escaping, but were made with holes wide enough apart so as to stretch the legs and bruise the feet causing great pain and injury. Their bodies were in excruciating pain. In spite of the agony, the Bible says at midnight, they prayed and sang praises unto God and the prisoners heard them. Obviously, they were singing and praying loud enough for others to hear. I even believe if their feet had not been in stocks, they would have danced all over that jail.

Something awesome happened while Paul and Silas were worshipping the Lord. The Bible says, suddenly, not the next day or two or three days later, but suddenly there was a a great earthquake, so that the foundations of the prison were shaken: and immediately all the doors were opened, and every one's bands were loosed. Paul and Silas, through prayer and praise invoked the power of God and not only were their bands loosed, but everybody's in the jail as well. The keeper of the prison awakened out of his sleep and seeing the prison doors open, he drew out his sword, to kill himself. He was responsible for the prisoners, under the penalty of death. He preferred to kill himself rather than face Roman punishment for the escape of the prisoners. Paul saw what he was about to do and cried with a loud voice, "Do thyself no harm, for we are all here." The jailer came in trembling, and fell down before Paul and

Silas saying, "Sirs, what must I do to be saved?" Paul and Silas experienced supernatural intervention because they made a decision to worship God in a difficult situation. Supernatural things always happen when man makes a decision to minister to the Lord, and live in consistent obedience to God. They even had an opportunity to minister salvation right there in the jail. What a magnificent display of the power of God. Ministering to the Lord also involves serving others.

Psalm 8:2
Out of the mouth of babes and sucklings hast thou ordained strength because of thine enemies, that thou mightest still the enemy and the avenger.

God has ordained praise to still the avenger. He has literally designed praise and worship to stop the forces of darkness. How is this done? The Bible says, God inhabits the praises of His people. Well if God abides in the praises of His people, when we praise and worship God, He fills the scene with His power and where He is present, the devil and all his cohorts, cannot stay. They must not only stop, but vacate the premises as well. Often we miss great opportunities to experience the supernatural move of God because we spend much too much time griping, criticizing others, murmuring and complaining, and not enough time worshipping God for who He is regardless of circumstances. We need to praise God for what He has already done. The Spirit of God says, *"Many manifestations of the power of God will become evident as we just dance before Him in worship."* We can dance ourselves right into victory.

II Samuel 6:14-15
*And David danced before the Lord with all
his might; and David was girded with a linen
ephod. So David and all the house of Israel
brought up the ark (symbolic of the presence
of God) of the Lord with shouting, and with
the sound of the trumpet.*

David danced before God with all his might. He had
on priestly garments, but this did not matter, his heart-felt
gratitude towards God for the victory he was experiencing
at that moment caused him to disregard circumstances and
worship his God (**II Samuel Chapter 6**).

The reason I believe phenomenal manifestations
are revealed in praise is because faith of this degree and
magnitude gets God's attention. Praise is the voice of faith
in God. It rejoices over the granted petition before the actual
manifestation. It rejoices over this truth, "Our God is God."

Psalm 90:1-4
*Lord, thou hast been our dwelling place in
all generations. Before the mountains were
brought forth, or ever thou hadst formed the
earth and the world, even from everlasting
to everlasting, thou art God. Thou turnest
man to destruction; and sayest, Return, ye
children of men. For a thousand years in thy
sight are but as yesterday when it is past, and
as a watch in the night.*

I must emphasize that I believe the prayer of praise and
worship is one of the highest forms of prayer. Man has to get
a vision of constantly overcoming in life. This type of praise

comes from the heart and in essence is faith in action. There are times when I believe God wants us just to spend time worshipping and praising Him. We spend hours planning programs of all sorts. We spend much time doing some really nice things, but there is a time that should be reserved for nothing but praise.

In **II Chronicles 20:1-24**, there was an occasion when Jehoshaphat faced a great army coming against him and his people. Jehoshaphat feared, set himself to seek God and proclaimed a fast throughout all Judah. He responded as many of us today. We become fearful and turn to God immediately for supernatural help. When we face adversity, we should turn to God in faith, not fear. In Jehoshaphat's fear, he said, "Lord, I have no might against this great company. My eyes are upon You." In essence Jehoshaphat was saying, "I am helpless; I must depend on God." He reminded God of all He had done and how he (Jehoshaphat) and the people of Judah had been obedient to what God had told them to do. God spoke through the prophet Jahaziel to tell the people of God, *"Be not afraid nor dismayed by reason of this great multitude; for the battle is not yours, but God's. Tomorrow go ye down against them: behold, they come up by the cliff of Ziz; and ye shall find them at the end of the brook, before the wilderness of Jeruel. Ye shall not need to fight in this battle: set yourselves, stand still, and see the salvation of the lord with you, O Judah and Jerusalem: fear not, nor be dismayed; tomorrow go ye out against them: <u>for the Lord will be with you.</u>"*

God revealed the strategy by which to overtake the enemy and exactly where the enemy was camped out. I believe if we will just praise and worship the Lord, God will give strategies to victory, reveal the enemy and where and how he seeks to destroy. I believe God will uncover the thing hidden, designed to hurt us. The people followed the instructions that came from the prophet of God. God gave the plan. All they had to do was follow the instructions. Immediately after the Word of the Lord came from the prophet, Jehoshaphat bowed his head with his face to the ground and all Judah and the inhabitants of Jerusalem fell before the Lord, worshipping the Lord. The Levites, of the children of the Kohathites, and the children of the Korhites, stood up to praise the Lord God of Israel with a loud voice on high. They rose early in the morning, and went forth into the wilderness of Tekoa and as they went forth, Jehoshaphat stood and said, *"Hear me O Judah, and ye inhabitants of Jerusalem; believe in the Lord your God so shall ye be established; believe his prophets so shall ye prosper. And when he had consulted with the people, he appointed singers unto the Lord, and that should praise the beauty of holiness, as they went out before the army, and to say Praise ye the Lord; for his mercy endureth for ever. And when they began to sing and to praise, the Lord sent ambushments against the children of Ammon, Moab and mount Seir, which were come against Judah and they were smitten. For the children of Ammon and Moab stood up against the inhabitants of mount Seir, utterly to slay and destroy them: and when they had made an end of the inhabitants of Seir every one helped to destroy another. All Judah went down to claim the spoils from the battle and the spoils were so plenteous it took three days to gather all."*

If we will minister to the Lord, I believe the blessings of God will rain upon us. As we praise the Lord we send confusion into the devil's camp. If you have been standing on the Word of God, yet you are facing battle after battle, it is time to minister to the Lord. Don't become weary in well-doing. Stay in a place of obedience. Refuse to be discouraged.

Galatians 6:9
And let us not be weary in well doing: for in due season we shall reap, if we faint not.

All throughout the Psalms, David speaks of dancing before the Lord, shouting and singing praise unto the Lord. He speaks of worshipping the Lord for His goodness, mercy and loving kindness. Oh, that men would praise the Lord.

Psalm 34:1-4
I Will bless the Lord at all times: his praise shall continually be in my mouth. My soul shall make her boast in the Lord: the humble shall hear thereof, and be glad. O magnify the Lord with me, and let us exalt his name together. I sought the Lord, and he heard me, and delivered me from all my fears.

The prayer of Praise and Worship gets God on the scene. It invokes the power and blessings of God. Crying, whining, and quoting scriptures will not bring God on the scene. Quoting the Word is important. It releases faith and the ability of God as we speak in line with God's Word. God is His Word. However, there are times when we need just to adore and treasure God as our Father. We need to just minister to Him. If we will minister to the Lord, He will always minister to us. He is the God who delivers, answers, protects, reveals the way out and so much more.

Psalm 33:1-4

Rejoice in the Lord, O ye righteous: for praise is comely for the upright. Praise the Lord with harp: sing unto him with the psaltery and an instrument of ten strings. Sing unto him a new song; play skilfully with a loud noise. For the word of the Lord is right; and all his works are done in truth.

Acts 13:2

As they ministered to the Lord and fasted the Holy Ghost said.....

Acts 4:31

And when they had prayed the place was shaken where they were assembled together; and they were all filled with the Holy Ghost and they spake the word of God with boldness.

Psalm 100:1-5

Make a joyful noise unto the Lord, all ye lands. Serve the Lord with gladness: come before his presence with singing. Know ye that the Lord he is God: it is he that hath made us, and not we ourselves; we are his people, and the sheep of his pasture. Enter into his gates with thanksgiving, and into his courts with praise: be thankful unto him, and bless his name. For the Lord is good; his mercy is everlasting; and his truth endureth to all generations.

Discerning the Father's Voice

*T*here is a hunger within every believer to understand God and to know God more personably. Not all believers are willing to do what is absolutely necessary to become intimately acquainted with God, but many do have the desire to communicate with Him more personably. God has given us the Holy Spirit to direct us into a spiritual awareness whereby we are able to examine (judge) what we hear and to distinguish between God's direction, man and satanic voices. As we abide in Him, and His Word abides in us, we are able to discern the voice of God, because, we are abiding in Him in obedience, and have grown accustomed to hearing His voice through, study of His Word, communion and fellowship. As we examine the scriptures we must be mindful that many, in an effort to understand the ways of God, have failed to realize that God is not mysterious and does not seek to bewilder His children. God is not trying to hide Himself from us. Time and time again the Bible reveals the desire of God to reveal Himself to His people. This revelation does not come independent of man doing something. As we learned earlier, revelation means to uncover, unveil, or reveal. God is knowable and has done all to reveal Himself to His people.

Ephesians 1:9

Having made known unto us the mystery of his will, according to his good pleasure which he hath purposed in himself.

It is God's will to reveal himself and his ways to his people. He is not mysterious. Perhaps His methods are not always understood, but according to His good pleasure He seeks to make known His will to all who earnestly seek Him.

James 4:4-10

Submit yourselves therefore to God, resist the devil and he will flee from you. Draw nigh to God and He will draw nigh to you. Cleanse your hands ye sinners; and purify your hearts, ye double mined. Be afflicted and mourn, and weep: let your laughter be turned to mourning, and your joy to heaviness. Humble yourselves in the sight of the Lord and he shall lift you up.

The secret to walking with God is found in man's willingness to submit to God. Submission refers to obedience to the Word of God in all manner of living and speaking. We must choose to resist anything and/or anyone that threatens our allegiance to God. God seeks to protect His children, however He can only protect us when we live within the confines of obedience to His Word. **Isaiah 1:19** says, *"If ye be willing and obedient, ye shall eat the good of the land."*

Psalm 50:15

Call upon me in the day of trouble: I will deliver thee and thou shalt glorify me.

God invites us to call upon Him in the day of trouble. He's not initiating the trouble, He simply says, "When you do encounter trouble call on the One who is well able to deliver you." Why does God want to deliver us? He clearly states that when we are delivered, it brings Him glory. He wants the world to know of His power to save, to heal, to deliver and set free those who trust in Him.

Psalm 99:6-8

Moses and Aaron among His priests, and Samuel among them that call upon his name; they called upon the Lord, and he answered them. He spake unto them in the cloudy pillar: they kept his testimonies, and the ordinance that he gave them. Thou answeredst them, O Lord our God: thou wast a God that forgavest them, though thou tookest vengeance of their inventions.

The patriarchs of old called upon God, and God answered them. There is something significant in these verses that will assist us in recognizing the Father's voice. Moses, Aaron and Samuel were positioned to hear from God. How do we know this? The above verses reveal that they kept God's testimonies and the ordinance He gave them. This indicates they were positioned in obedience. I did not say they never made a mistake, nor does the scripture. It simply says they were obedient to the Word of the Lord. Many want to hear the audible voice of God, enjoy the blessings of God, and operate in the gifts of the Spirit, but do not want to live right before God or His people. Once again, there is a price to pay to receive from God. Man cannot live anyway he chooses, mistreat and slander others and still expect to live in God's best. God longs to answer His people and direct their lives. The following scriptures reveal that it is the will of God to direct His people and answer their cry:

141

Isaiah 65:24

And it shall come to pass, that before they call, I will answer; and while they are yet speaking, I will hear.

God says before we call upon Him, He will answer. Why? Because He already knows what we have need of before we ask; and while we are speaking He hears. God receives glory and honor when we receive answers to our prayers. God welcomes the opportunity to respond to our prayers.

Jeremiah 33:1-3

Moreover the Word of the Lord came unto Jeremiah the second time, while he was yet shut up in the court of the prison, saying, thus saith the Lord the maker thereof, the Lord that formed it, to establish it; the Lord is his name; call unto me, and I will answer thee, and shew thee great and mighty things, which thou knowest not.

Psalm 91:14-15

Because he hath set his love upon me, therefore will I deliver him: I will set him on high, because he hath known my name. He shall call upon me, and I will answer him: I will be with him in trouble; I will deliver him, and honor him. With long life will I satisfy him, and shew him my salvation.

These are only a few of the scriptures that reveal God's invitation to His children to call upon Him and His willingness not only to answer, but deliver as well. In previous chapters we have discussed how God vows to deliver the man who sets his affection upon the God of the Universe (**Psalm 91:14-15**). God says those who love Him more than all else, those who commit to know His name because they have spent time in His presence, these are the ones who when they cry out, He says, My arm is stretched out mightily to deliver.

Psalm 118:5
I called upon the Lord in distress: the Lord
answered me and set me in a large place.

In these last days it is vital that believers long to hear the Father's voice. In many religious circles, believers have become dependent upon the prophet to hear from God. While I certainly believe in the ministry of the prophet and the gift of prophecy, I do not believe any child of God should be dependent on a word of prophecy to govern his or her life. This is dangerous, and many have fallen prey to devastating consequences when their lives were ruled by a prophetic word. Many believers attend specific services solely for the purpose of hearing a word from the prophet. The word of the prophet should direct the people to God, and confirm what God has already said to you. It should confirm a truth God has already revealed to the particular person or persons. God does not direct our lives by a word of prophecy, by way of the ministry of the prophet. The following scripture should be established in the heart of every believer:

II Peter 1:19-21
We have also a more sure word of prophecy;
whereunto ye do well that ye take heed, as
unto a light that shineth in a dark place,
until the day dawn, and the day star arise
in your hearts: Knowing this first, that no

prophecy of the scripture is of any private interpretation. For the prophecy came not in old time by the will of man: but holy men of God spake as they were moved by the Holy Ghost.

Hebrews 1:1-2
God, who at sundry times and in divers manners spake in time past unto the fathers by the prophets, <u>hath in these last days spoken unto us by His Son (The Word), whom he hath appointed heir of all things, by whom also he made the worlds.</u>

The primary way God speaks to us today is by His written Word. The Bible is a more sure word of prophecy, given to us by God. It reveals the love of God, the nature and character of God; it reveals who we are and the benefits we enjoy because of who we are. The Bible reveals our enemy, what is to be expected of him, and the authority we possess in this earth over the enemy. The Bible reveals the plan of God for all humanity. Peter admonishes believers to take heed to the written Word. He says it is like light shining in a dark place. It is like the dawning of day as it brings enlightenment and understanding. Timothy tells us that the written Word is inspired by God and it is our responsibility to ***study the written Word***. The Bible is God speaking to His children. We hear God speak every time we read the Bible.

Psalm 19:7-8
The law of the Lord is perfect, <u>converting (transforming) the soul</u>: the testimony of the Lord is sure, making wise the simple. The

statutes of the Lord are right, rejoicing the heart: the commandment of the Lord is pure, enlightening the eyes.

Psalm 119:4-16

Thou hast commanded us to keep thy precepts diligently. O that my ways were directed to keep thy statues! Then shall I not be ashamed, when I have respect unto all thy commandments. I will praise thee with uprightness of heart, when I shall have learned thy righteous judgments. I will keep thy statutes: O forsake me not utterly. <u>Wherewithal shall a young man cleanse his way? By taking heed thereto according to thy Word.</u> With my whole heart have I sought thee: O let me not wander from thy commandments. <u>Thy word have I hid in mine heart, that I might not sin against thee.</u> Blessed art thou, O Lord: teach me thy statutes. With my lips have I declared all the judgments of thy mouth. I have rejoiced in the way of thy testimonies, as much as in all riches. I will meditate in thy precepts, and have respect unto thy ways. I will delight myself in thy statutes: <u>I will not forget thy word.</u>

God also speaks to us through our Pastor. Every believer should be submitted to, committed to, firmly fixed in and attached to a local church. It is through our Pastor that God will direct us and protect us. The Pastor will feed God's people with knowledge and understanding. The gender of the Pastor does not matter. ***<u>What the Pastor teaches and how the Pastor lives, does matter</u>***.

Jeremiah 3:15

And I will give you <u>pastors, (male or female)</u>
according to mine heart, which shall feed you
with knowledge and understanding.

Matthew 16:18

That thou appear not unto men to fast, but
unto thy Father which is in secret: and thy
Father, which seeth in secret, shall reward
thee openly.

Many believers are not able to distinguish the Father's
voice because of their lack of study in the Word of God.
They are not committed to a local church, and are dependent
on others to hear from God for them. For this reason many
are deceived, led astray, and some have retarded their own
spiritual development. God is speaking today and He desires
to give every believer direction and insight in every area
of life. It is not the will of God that we be dependent on
other believers just to get a word to us. ***God wants to speak
directly to you through the Bible***. He is more concerned
about you overcoming life's challenges, than you are. God is
more concerned about you having clear direction in life, than
you are. However, God will not speak apart from His Word,
because He is His Word and He has exalted His Word above
His name. The Spirit and the Word always agree. If God
reveals a word to our spirits, that word will always agree
with the Bible, the written Word, the Logos.

God has given us His Word so that we can clearly discern
His voice. Listening to the Father's voice is at the heart of
our communication with God. We train our spirit to hear
from God as we acquaint ourselves with His Word. We must
become acquainted with the language by which He speaks.

The more we acquaint ourselves with the Word of God the better able we are to discern His voice. As we saturate ourselves with His Word, there will be times when He simply whispers to us and we know we have heard His voice because we have familiarized ourselves with the language by which He speaks. He will never speak a thing that is contradictory to His written Word, the Logos, the Bible. We may never hear an audible voice, dream a dream, or see a vision, but we can always hear God as we read the Bible.

The scripture refers to the importance of the written Word. The Bible is the "Logos" or written Word of God. As we study the scriptures and meditate in them day and night, we come to understand how God leads his children. ***God is not mysterious***. He has freely given us His Word in order that we might be wise in our dealings with Him and with others. ***God has freely given us Pastors to assist us in our growth***.

John 10:25-27

Jesus answered them, I told you, and ye believed not: the works that I do in my Father's name, they bear witness of me. But ye believe not, because ye are not of my sheep, as I said unto you. My sheep hear my voice and I know them, and they follow me:

There are other methods by which God speaks to His people but all should be verified by the Bible. In order to deal with these methods in great detail, one would have to go through the scriptures and distinctly analyze them. I will not do this in this book. I will simply share with you the other methods and provide scripture reference. Be aware, we hear one of three voices: God's voice, satan's voice, or our own human spirit. In order for us to discern which voice is speaking, we must be skilled in our knowledge of the written Word and we must have some experiences with God.

Another avenue God uses to speak to his people is through the gifts of the Spirit (**I Corinthians 12:1-31**). These gifts operate only as the Spirit wills and are primarily prophecy, a word of wisdom, a word of knowledge or tongues and interpretation of tongues.

- God can speak through an audible voice (**Acts 9:7**), or a still small voice (**I Kings 19:12**).
- God speaks through dreams and visions (**Acts 9:10**; **Acts 2:17**; **Acts 16:9**), or angels (**Matthew 1:20**).
- God speaks through an inward witness or impression (**I John 5:10**; **Romans 8:16**; **II Corinthians 2:13**).

He has many ways of communicating with us. His Best and most common way is the Bible, which is God speaking to men. Members of the Body of Christ can be spokesmen by which God speaks to his people, but test all things by the written Word, (**I John 4:1-4**).

Regardless of how God chooses to get a message to us, He never speaks apart from His Word. God's Word is plain and simple. It comes to bring direction, not confusion. This is why it is imperative that every believer is a serious student of the Word of God and committed to a Bible-believing, Bible-teaching church. God wants us to have full knowledge, and this only comes through intimacy with God.

We cannot hear what the Spirit is speaking, unless, we have a hearing ear and a heart open to obey God. We must have a will to hear the voice of God and be willing to obey

His voice. ***We do possess the capacity to hear from God***. People come to me all the time to ask how can I know I have heard from God or how do I discern the voice of God. I take them right back to the written Word of God, the "Logos." I explain the importance of spending time in the Word of God through study and faithful attendance in their local church. People who tell me God never speaks to them are telling me, they don't read the Word, they definitely don't attend church and they are not submitted to their Pastor; because God's Word, once again, is God speaking to His people.

If you are reading your Bible daily, God is speaking to you daily. If you have a Pastor, in each service, God uses that Pastor to speak to His people. Members of our church constantly tell me how God gave them direction, answers, hope and comfort through the sermons I preach. There are times when we have become so fat, or full of the Word until when a "Rhema" Word comes, we immediately verify it by scripture. "Rhema", is the Greek word for the spoken or revealed Word of God. God will deal directly with a particular individual regarding a particular situation. When we allow God's Word to dwell in us richly, it will rise up within us and speak to us. When we lie down it speaks to us; while on the job, in the car, in the shower, while traveling on the highway or preparing dinner; God will speak to us all day long when we have ears to hear.

Colossians 3:16
Let the word of Christ dwell in you richly in all wisdom; teaching and admonishing one another in psalms and hymns and spiritual songs, singing with grace in your hearts to the Lord.

149

The more time we spend with God, the more we come to understand His speech and His way. The Word and wisdom of God will rise up in you and me before we realize it, we have the answer. God has made our bodies' His dwelling place and we have His mind in every situation of life. He will expose satan's voice with His Word. He will expose our flesh with His Word.

John 8:42-47

Jesus said unto them, If God were your Father, ye would love me, for I proceeded forth and came from God; neither came I of myself, but he sent me. Why do ye not understand my speech? Even because ye cannot hear my word. Ye are of your father the devil, and the lusts of your father ye will do. He was a murderer from the beginning, and abode not in the truth, because there is no truth in him. When he speaketh a lie, he speaketh of his own: for he is a liar, and the father of it. And because I tell you the truth, ye believe me not. Which of you convinceth me of sin? And if I say the truth, why do ye not believe me? He that is of God heareth God's words: ye therefore hear them not, because ye are not of God.

I Corinthians 2:14:16

But the natural man receiveth not the things of the Spirit of God: for they are foolishness unto him: neither can he know them, because they are spiritually discerned. But he that is spiritual judgeth all things, yet he himself is judged of no man. For who hath known the mind of the Lord, that he may instruct him? But we have the mind of Christ.

I John 2:14:16
I have written unto you, fathers, because ye have known him that is from the beginning. I have written unto you, young men, because ye are strong, and the word of God abideth in you, and ye have overcome the wicked one. Love not the world, neither the things that are in the world. If any man love the world, the love of the Father is not in him. For all that is in the world, the lust of the flesh, and the lust of the eyes, and the pride of life, is not of the Father, but is of the world.

www.ingramcontent.com/pod-product-compliance
Lightning Source LLC
Chambersburg PA
CBHW031514040426
42445CB00009B/217